Zone Eleven

Mike Mandel

PHOTOGRAPHS BY
Ansel Adams

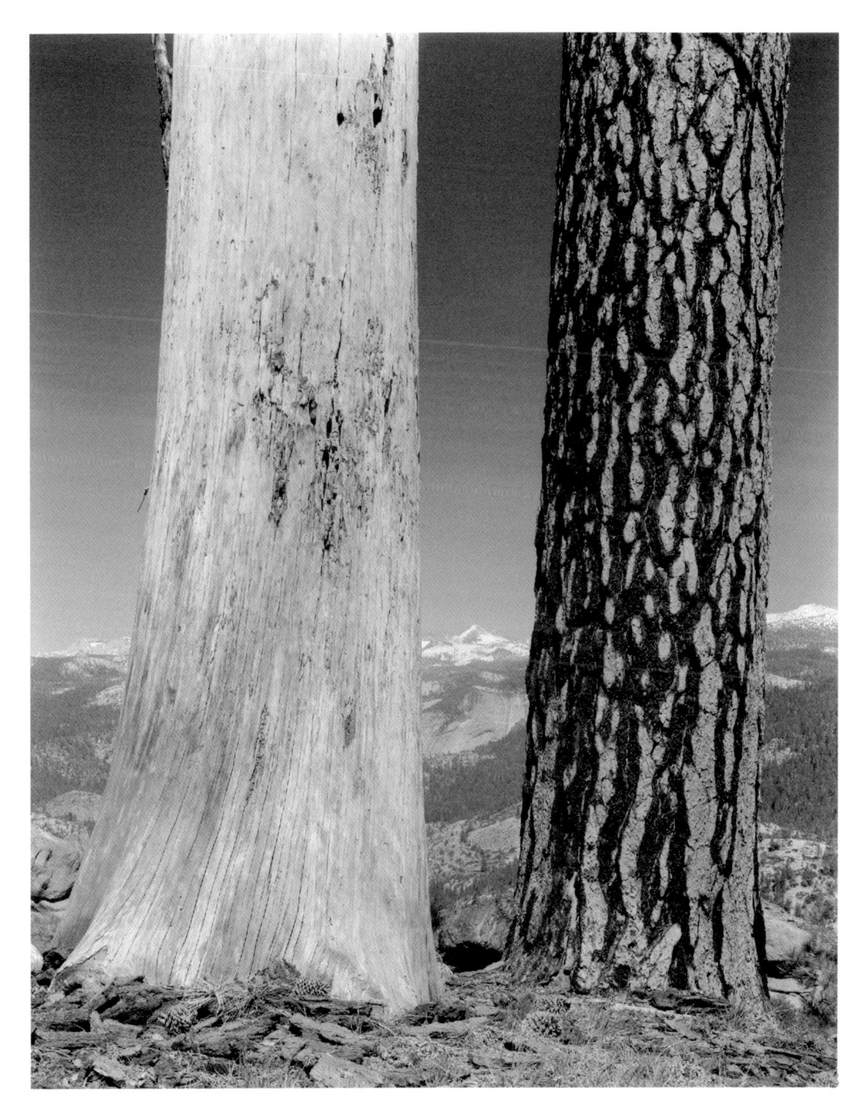

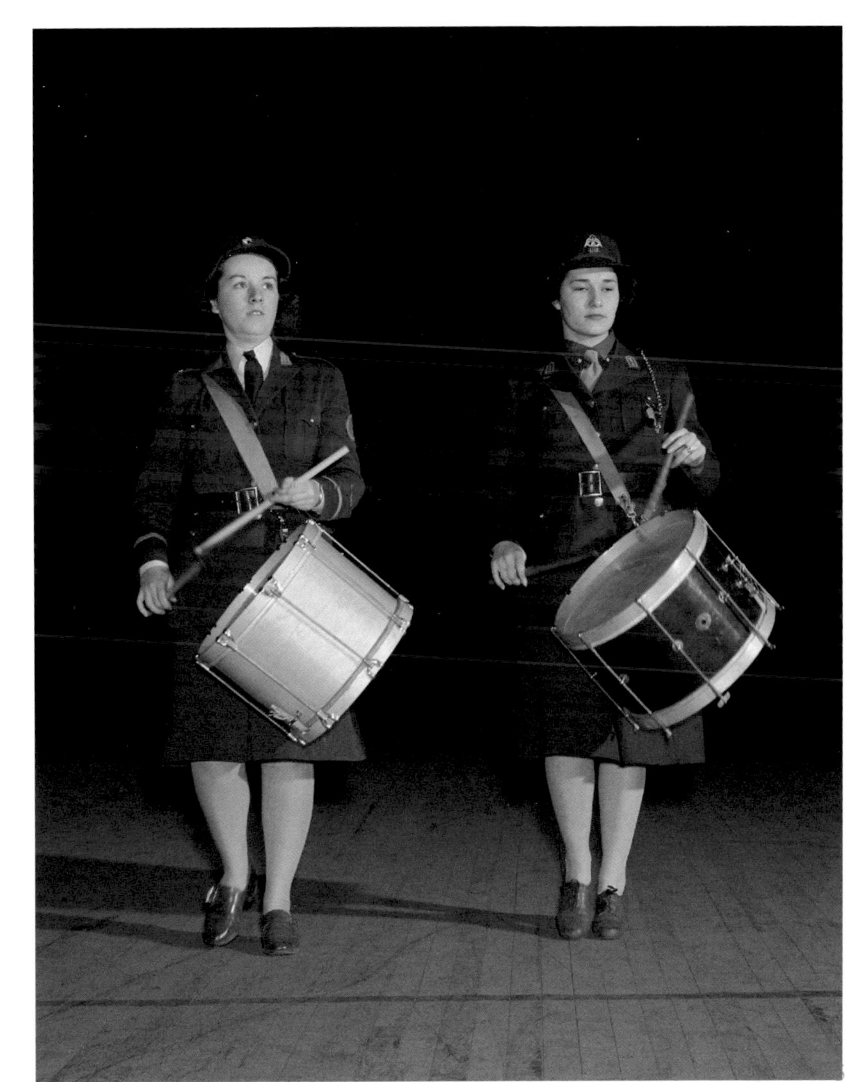

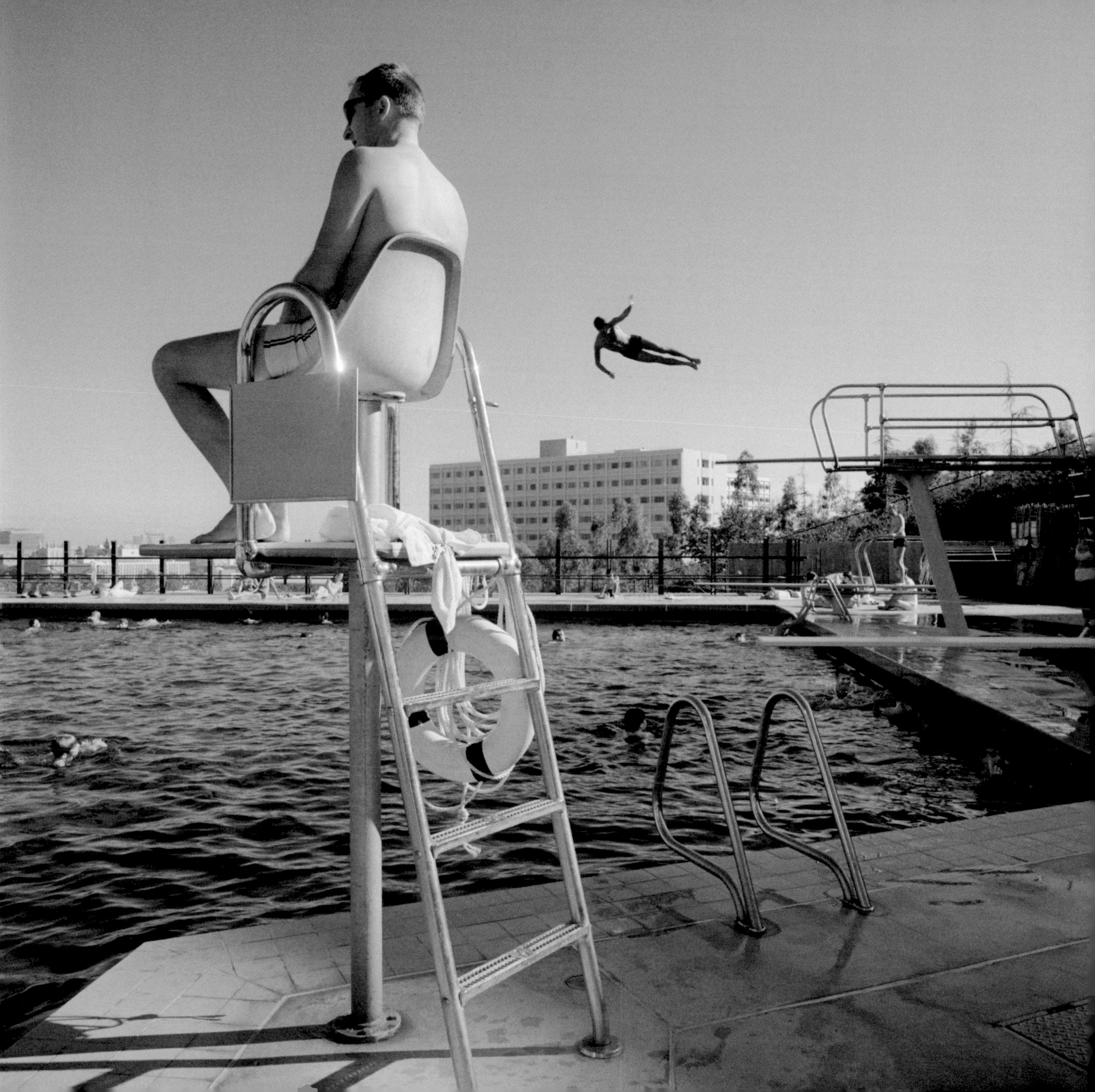

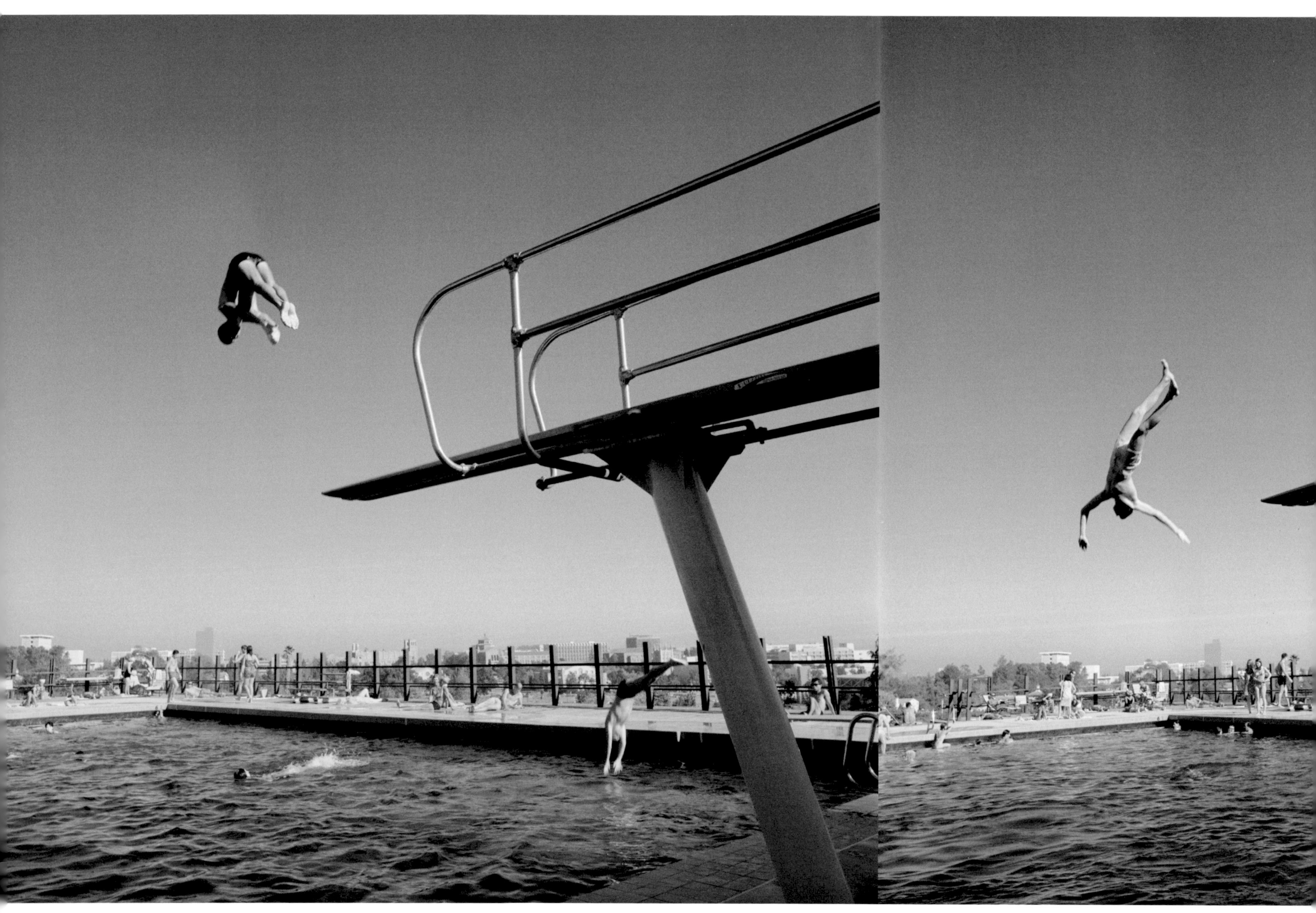

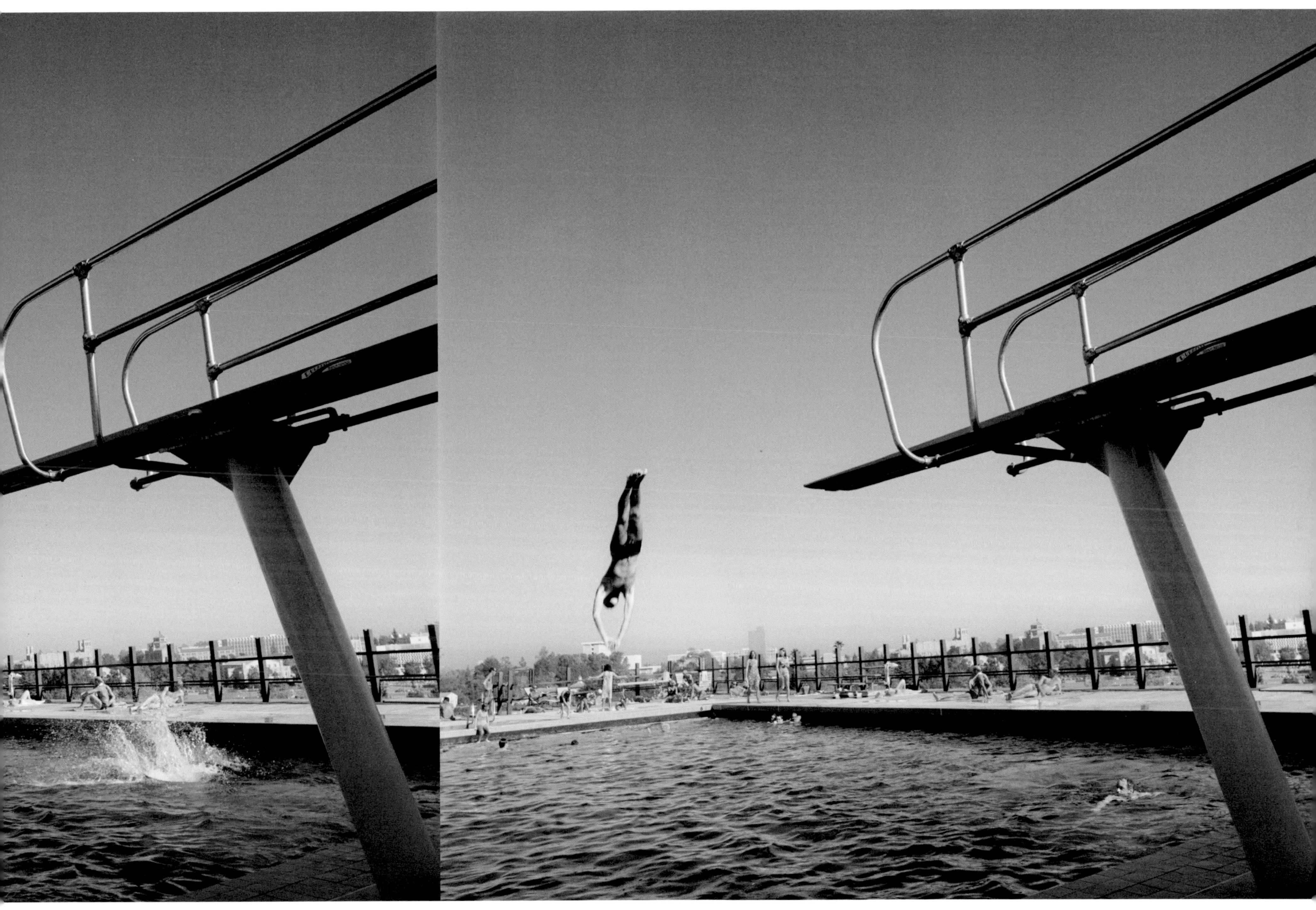

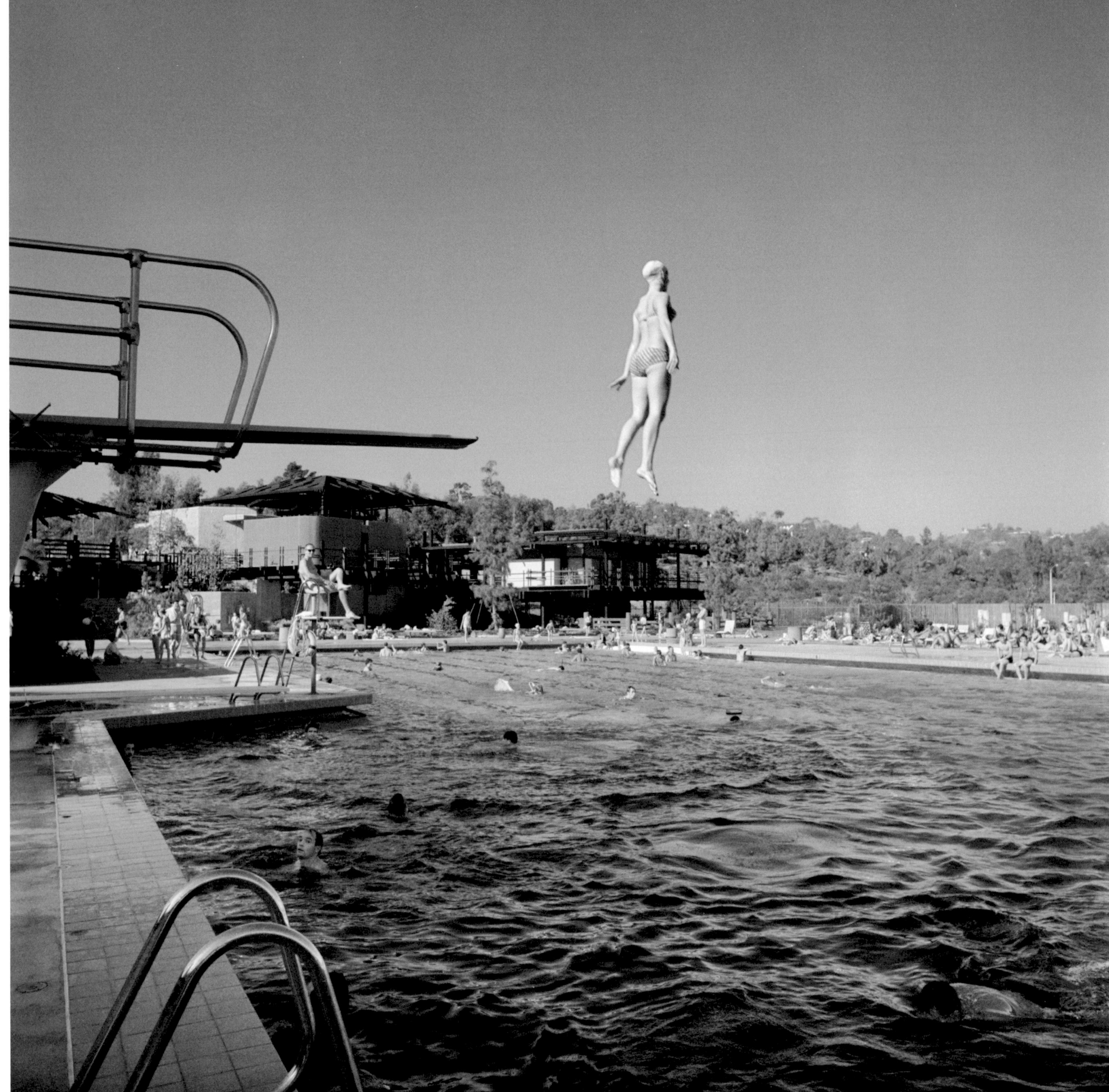

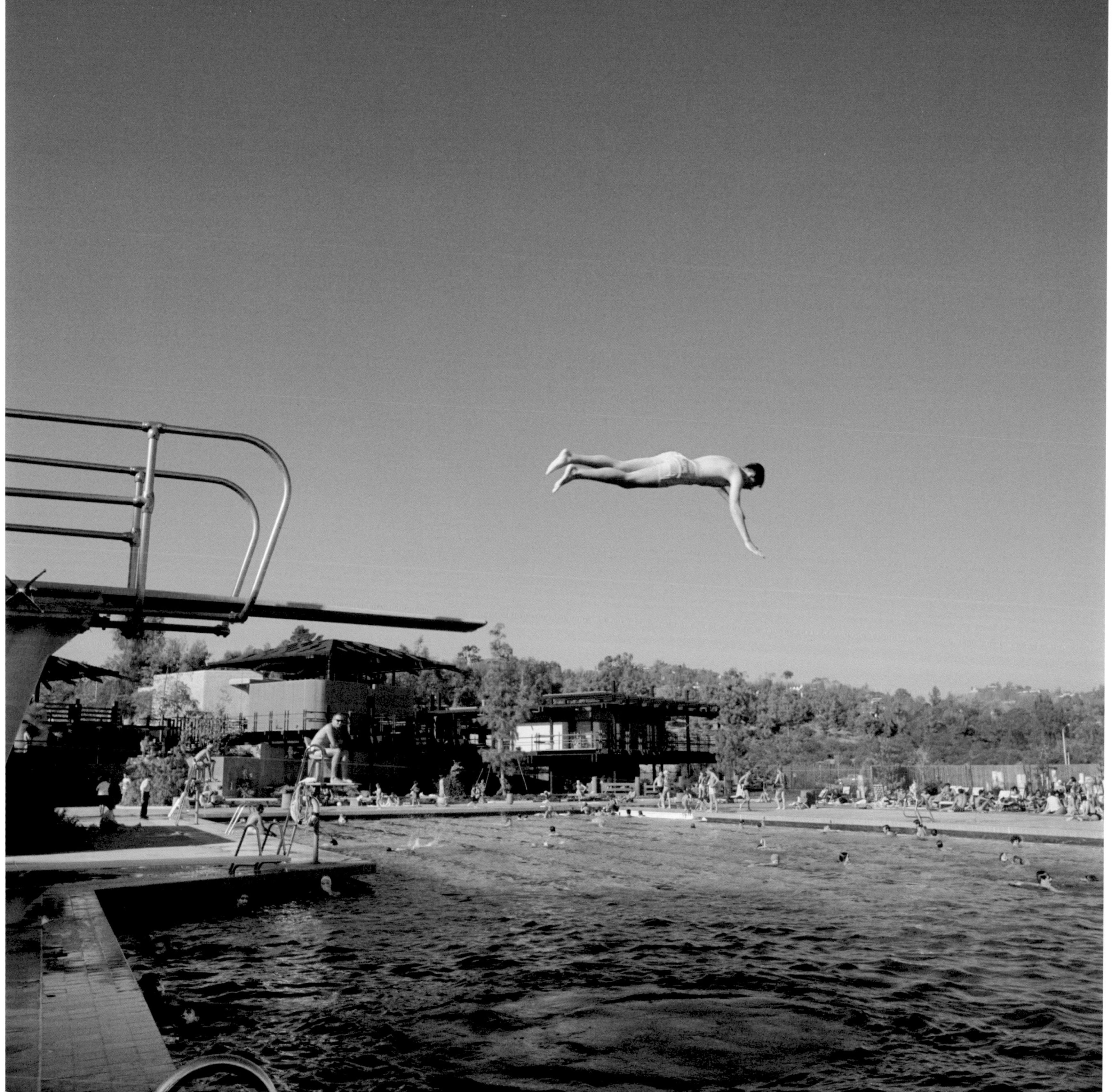

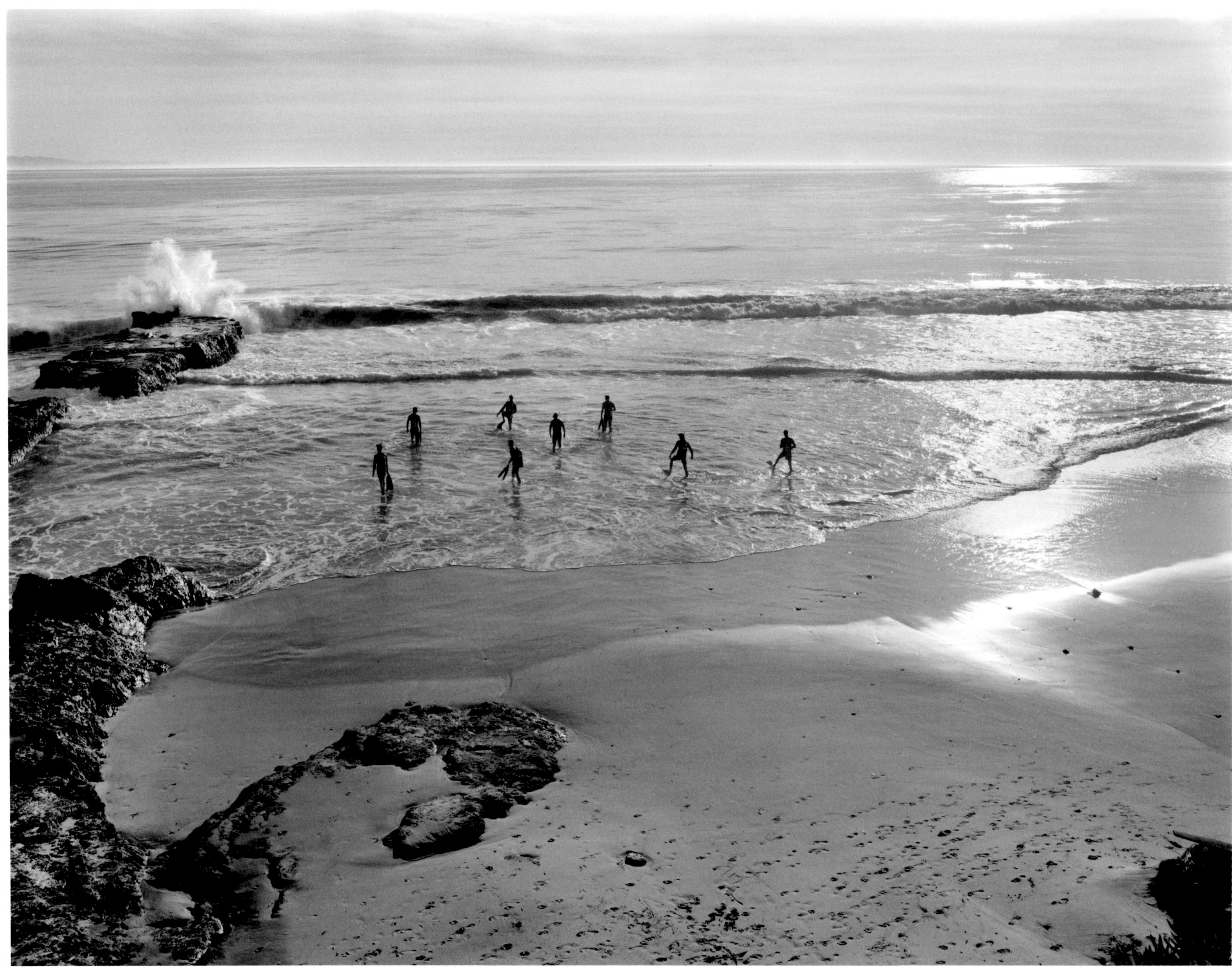

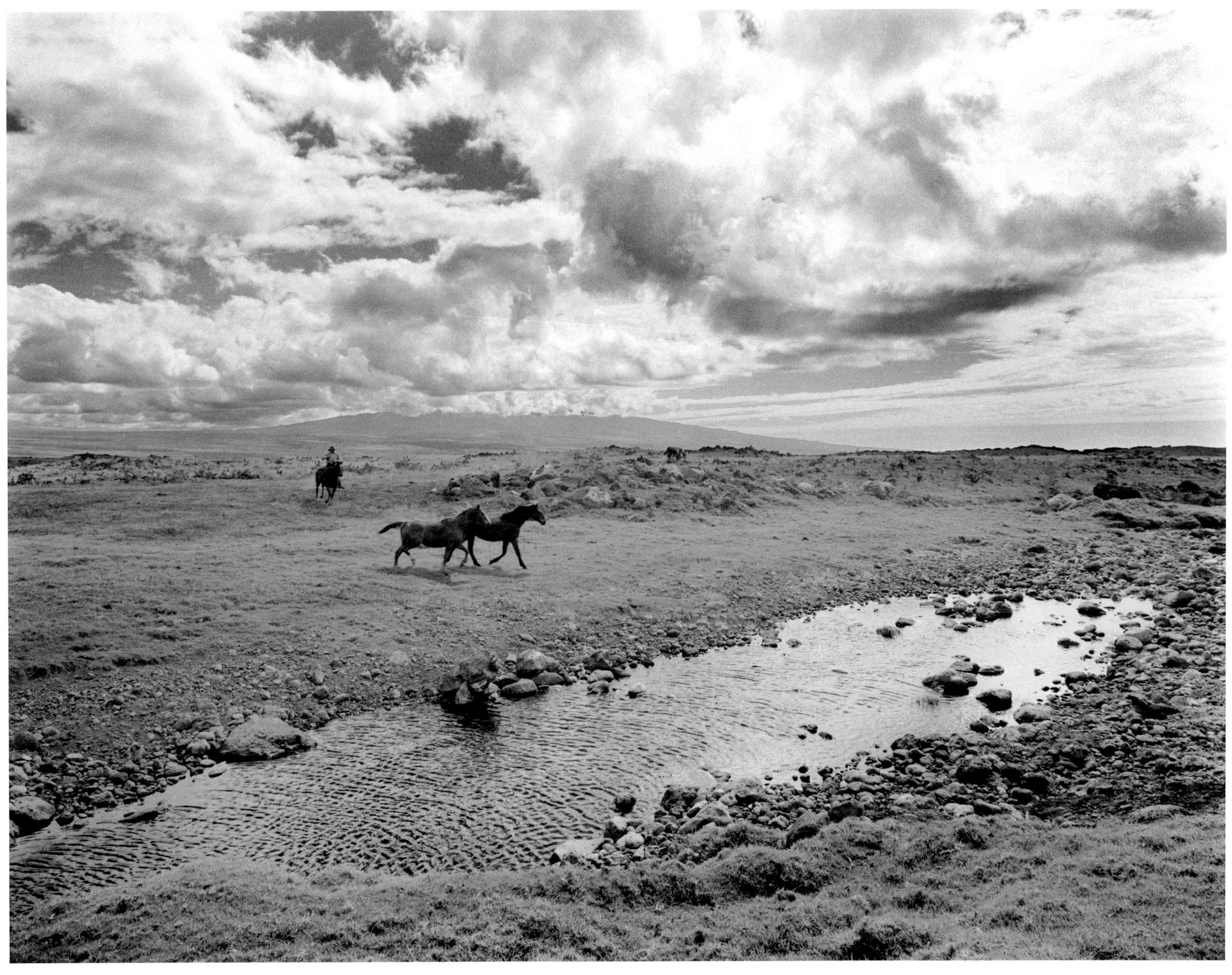

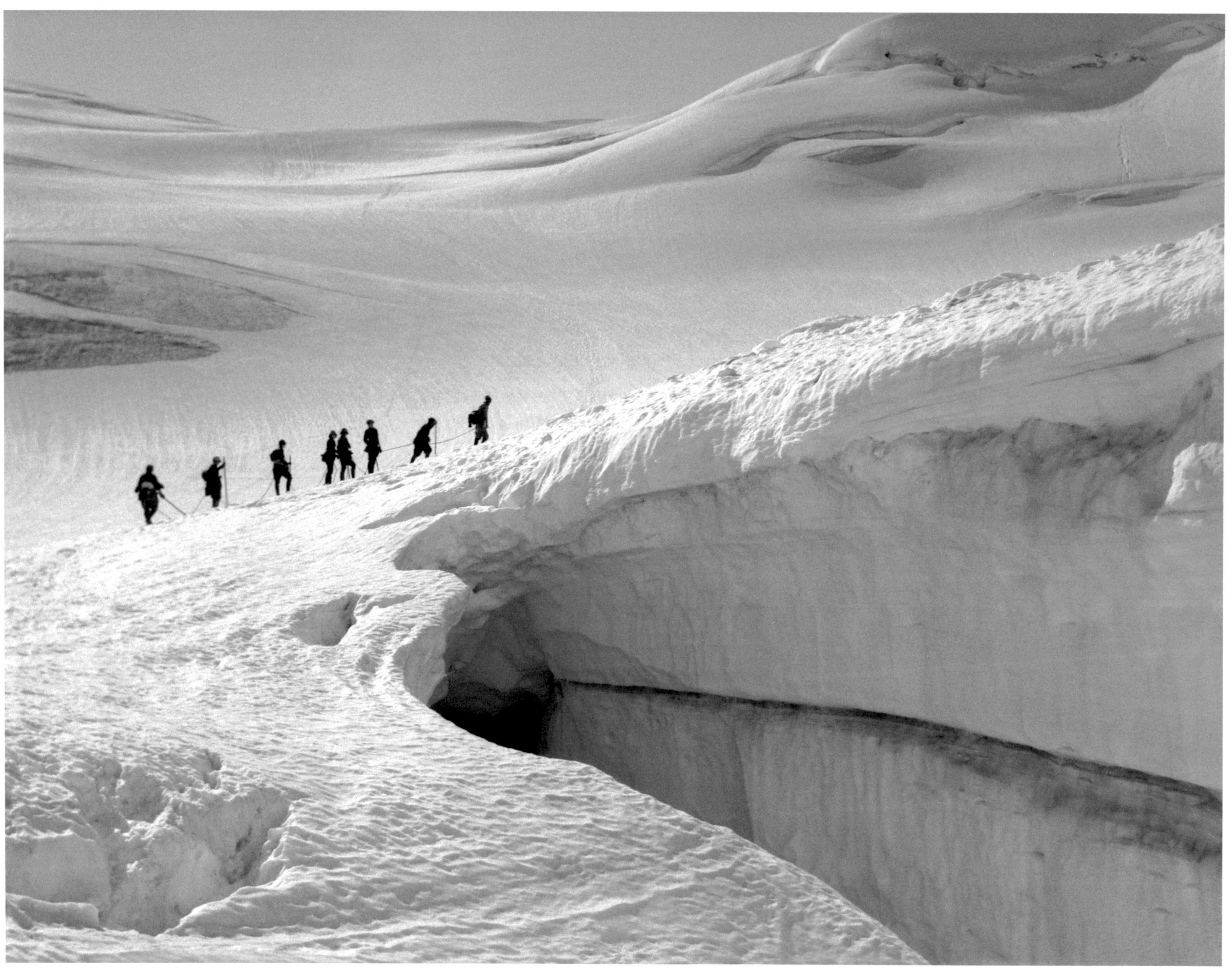

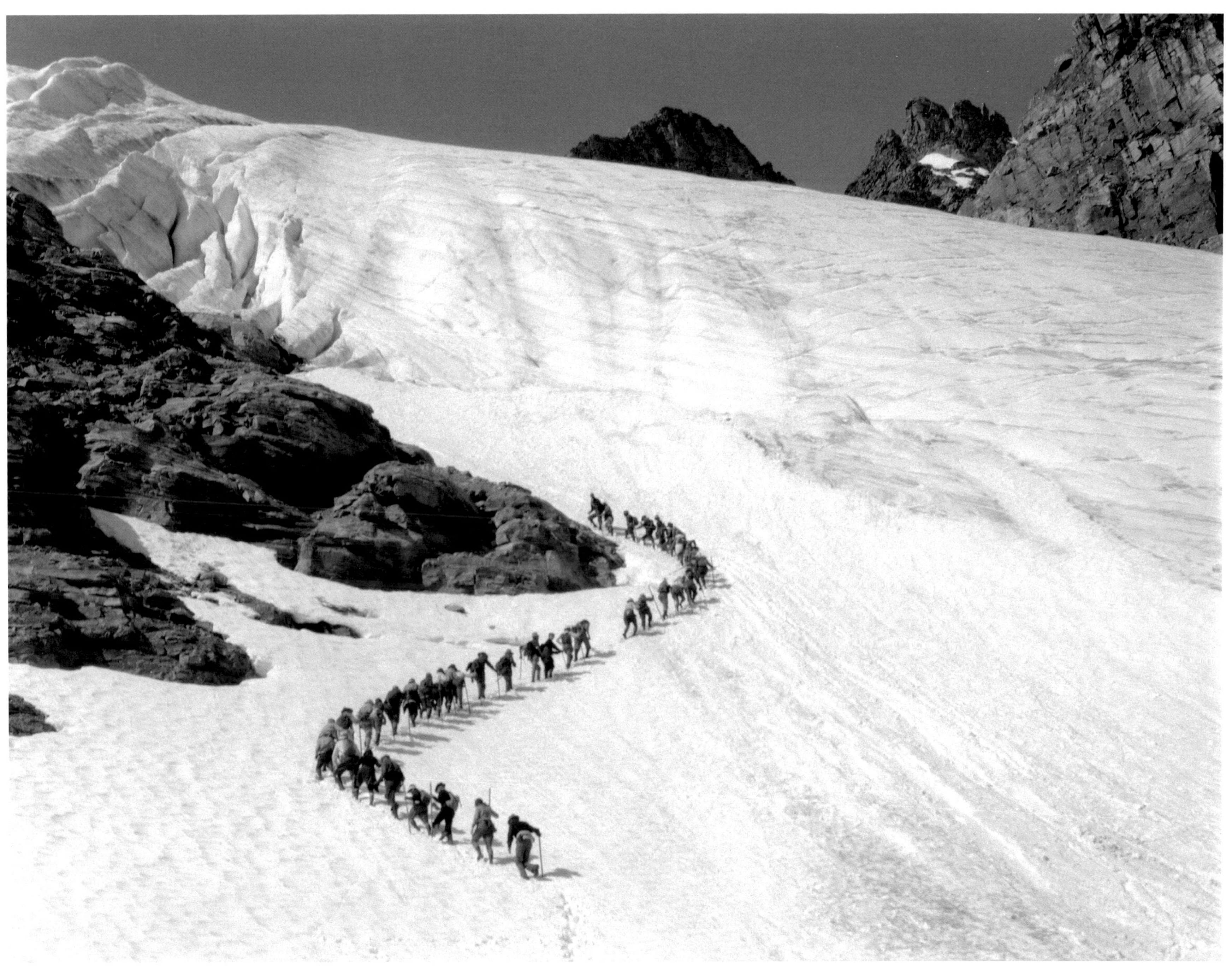

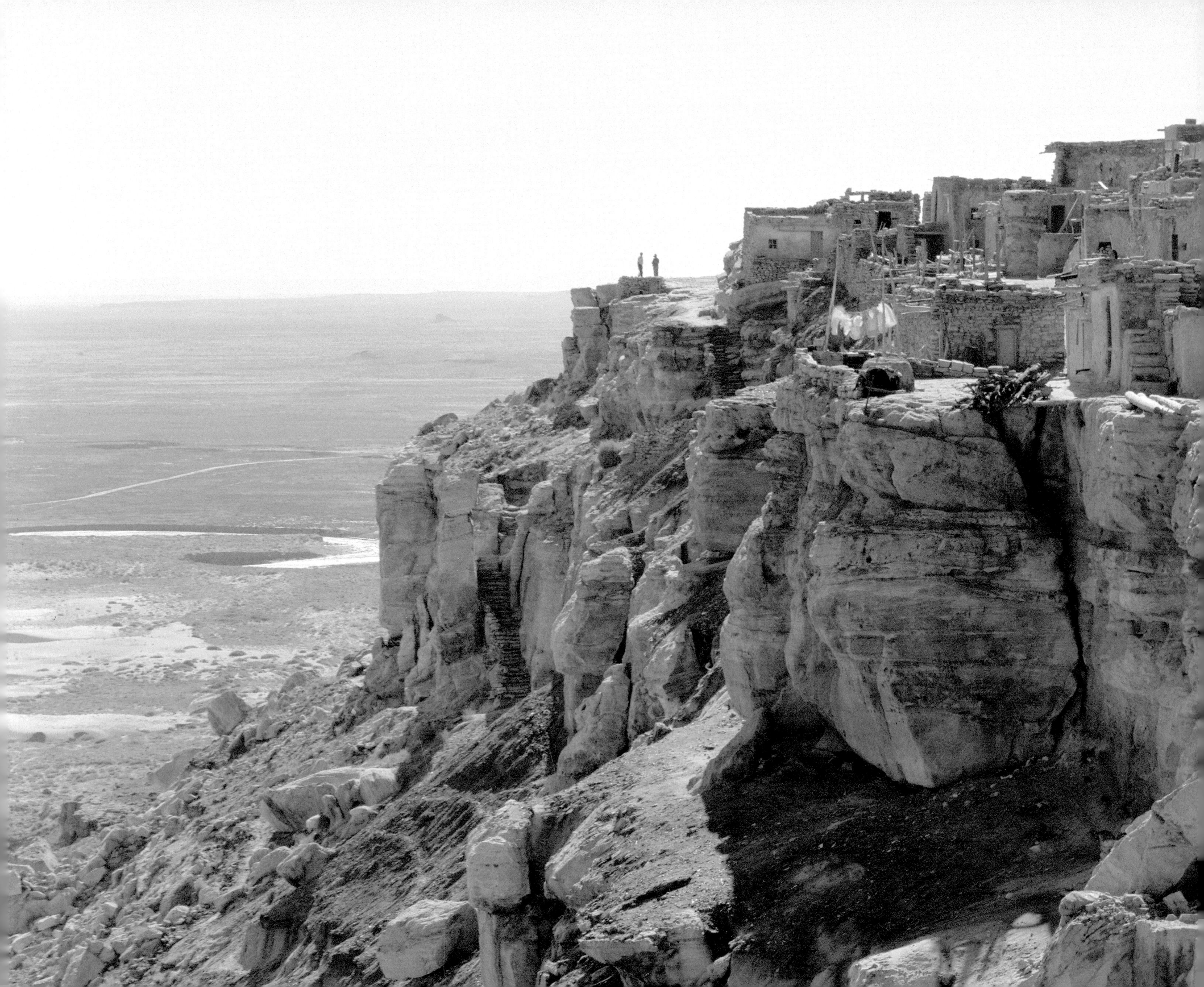

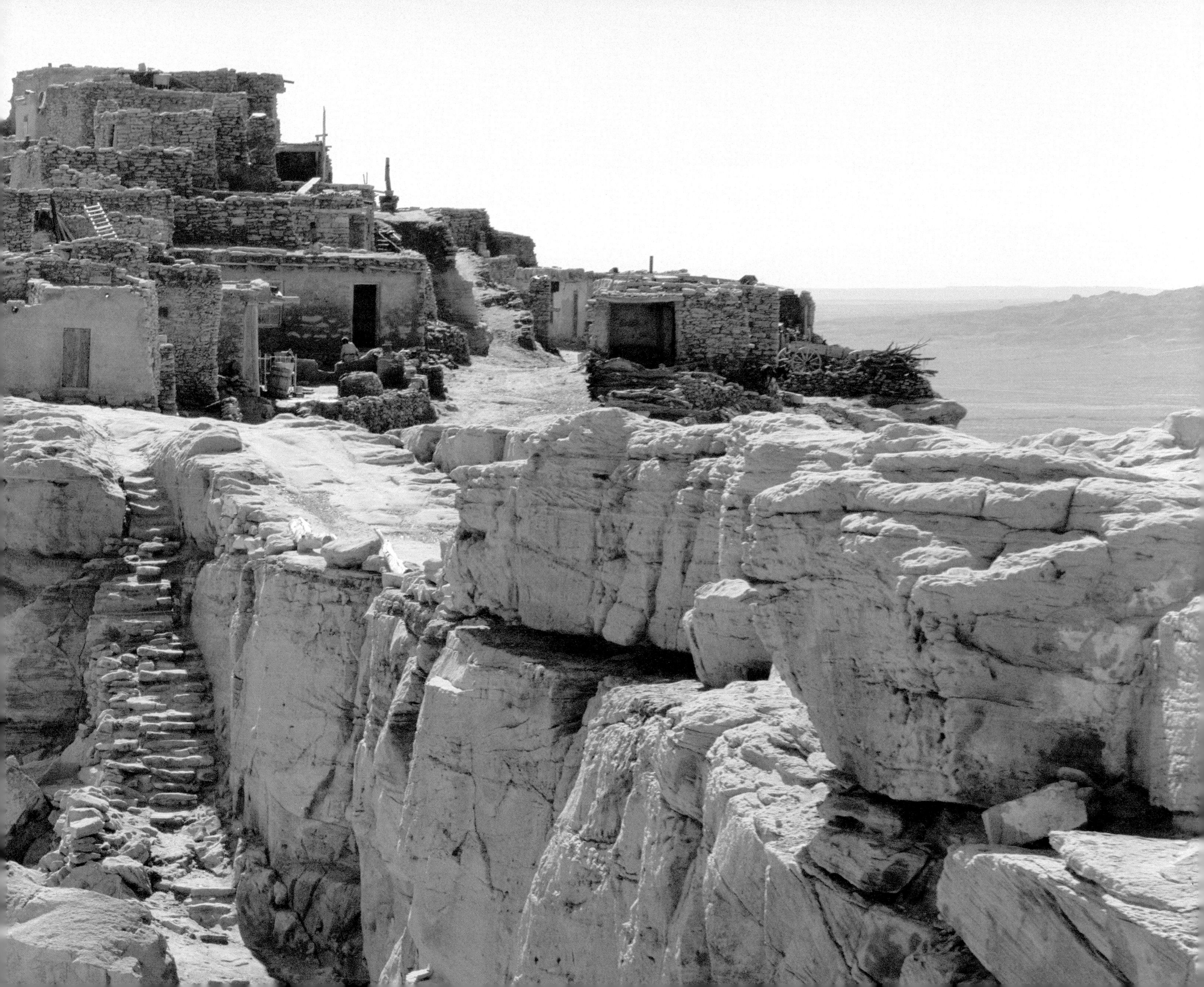

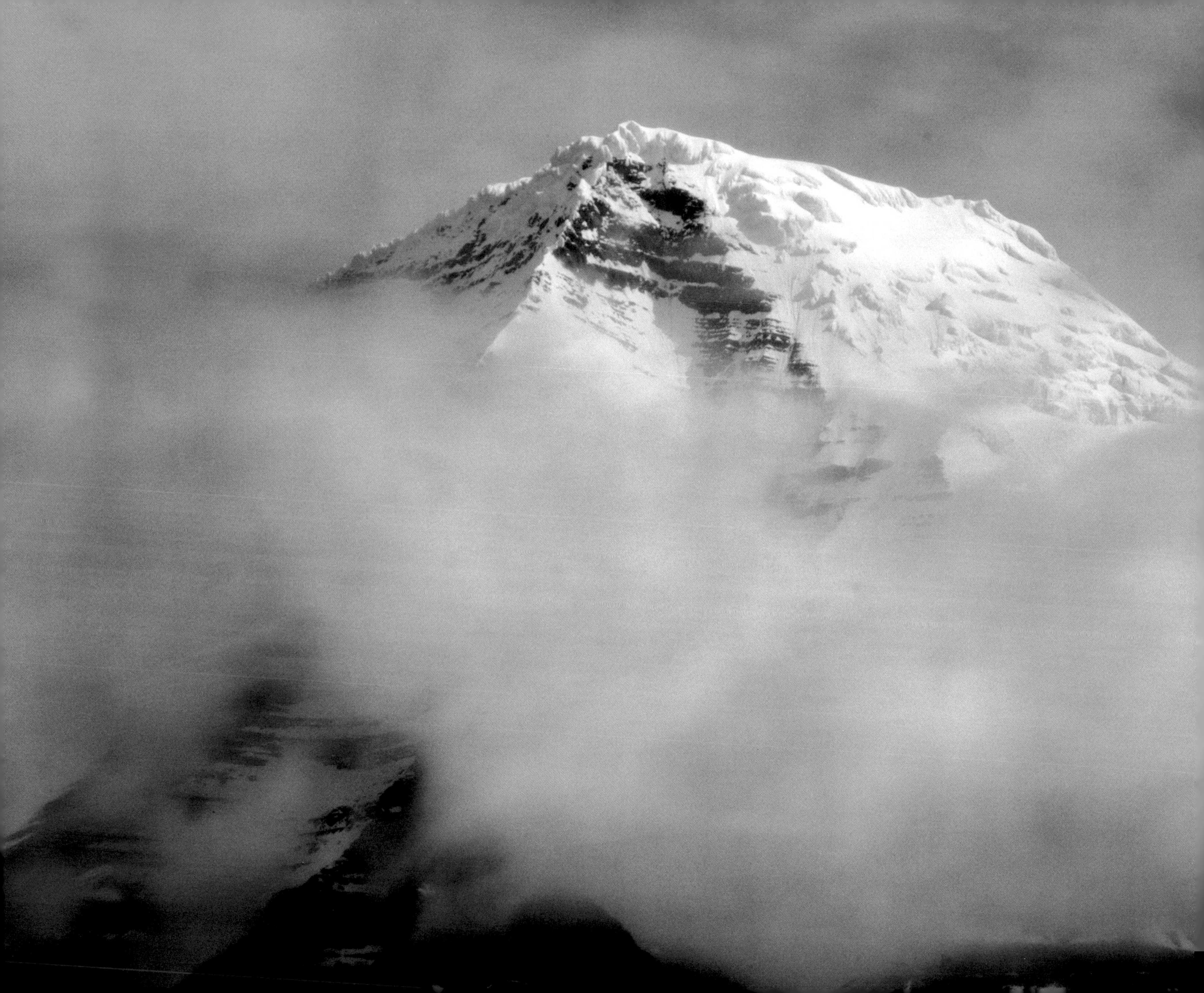

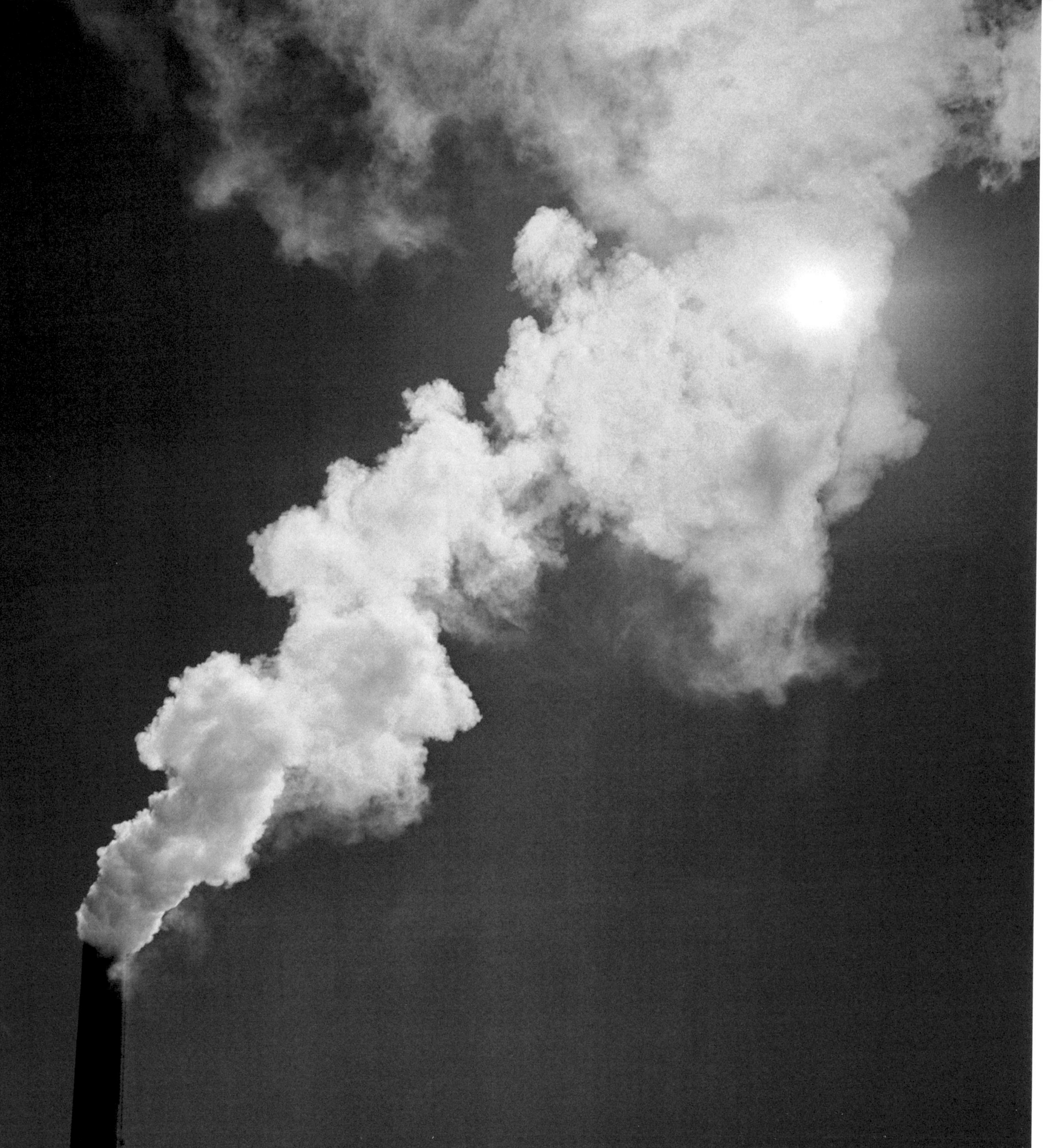

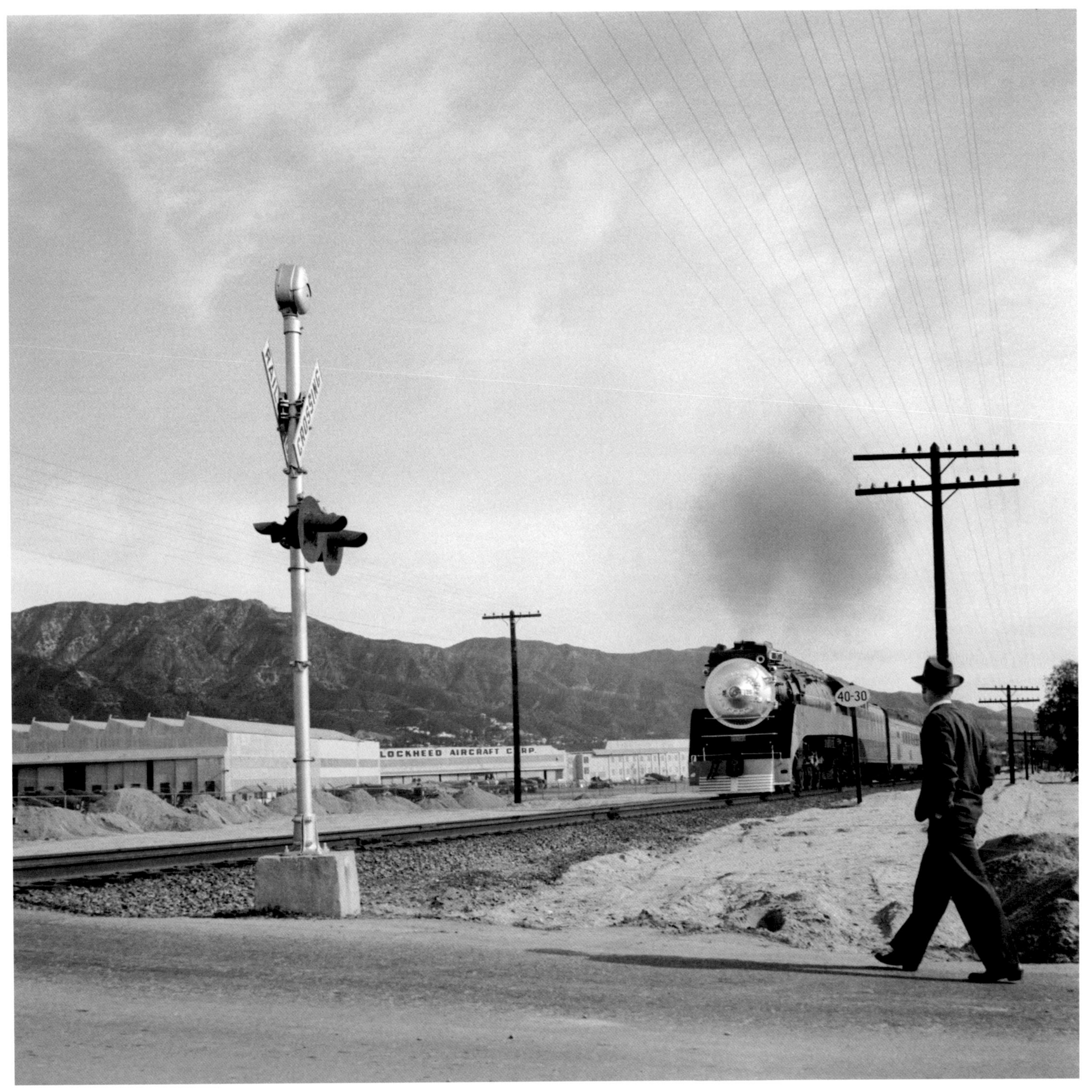
RAIL
CROSSING
LOCKHEED AIRCRAFT CORP.
40-30

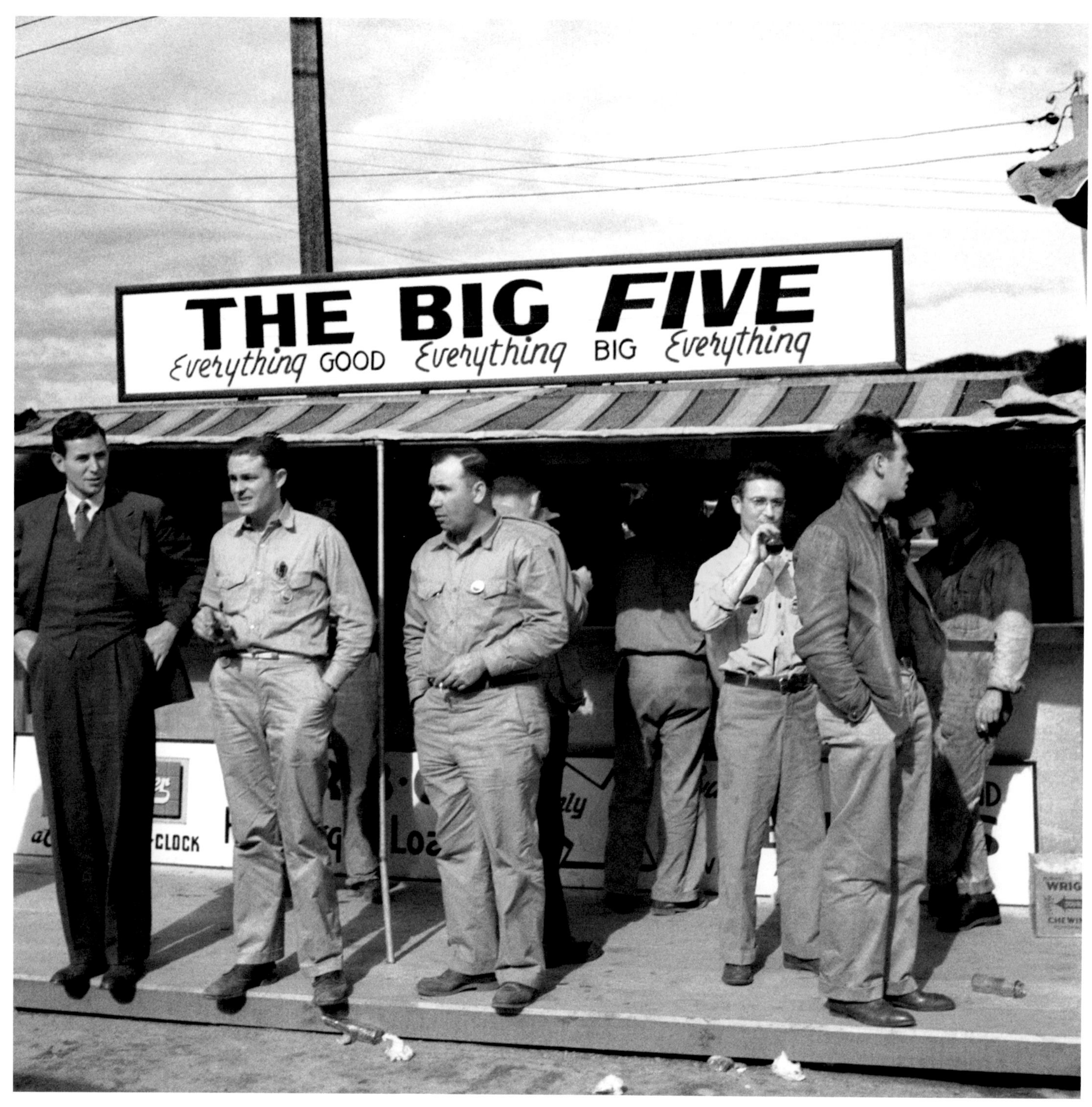

22

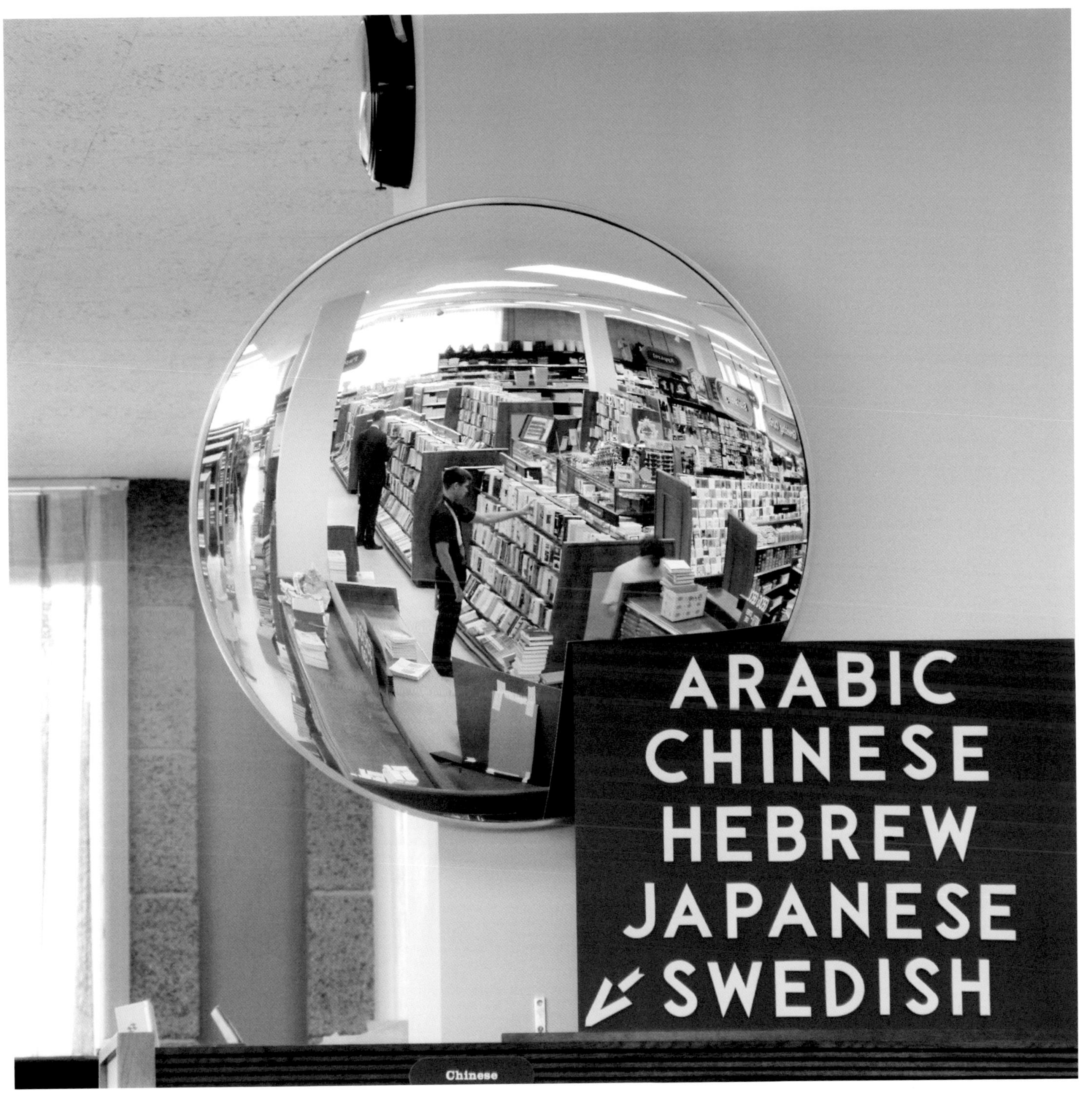
ARABIC
CHINESE
HEBREW
JAPANESE
SWEDISH
Chinese

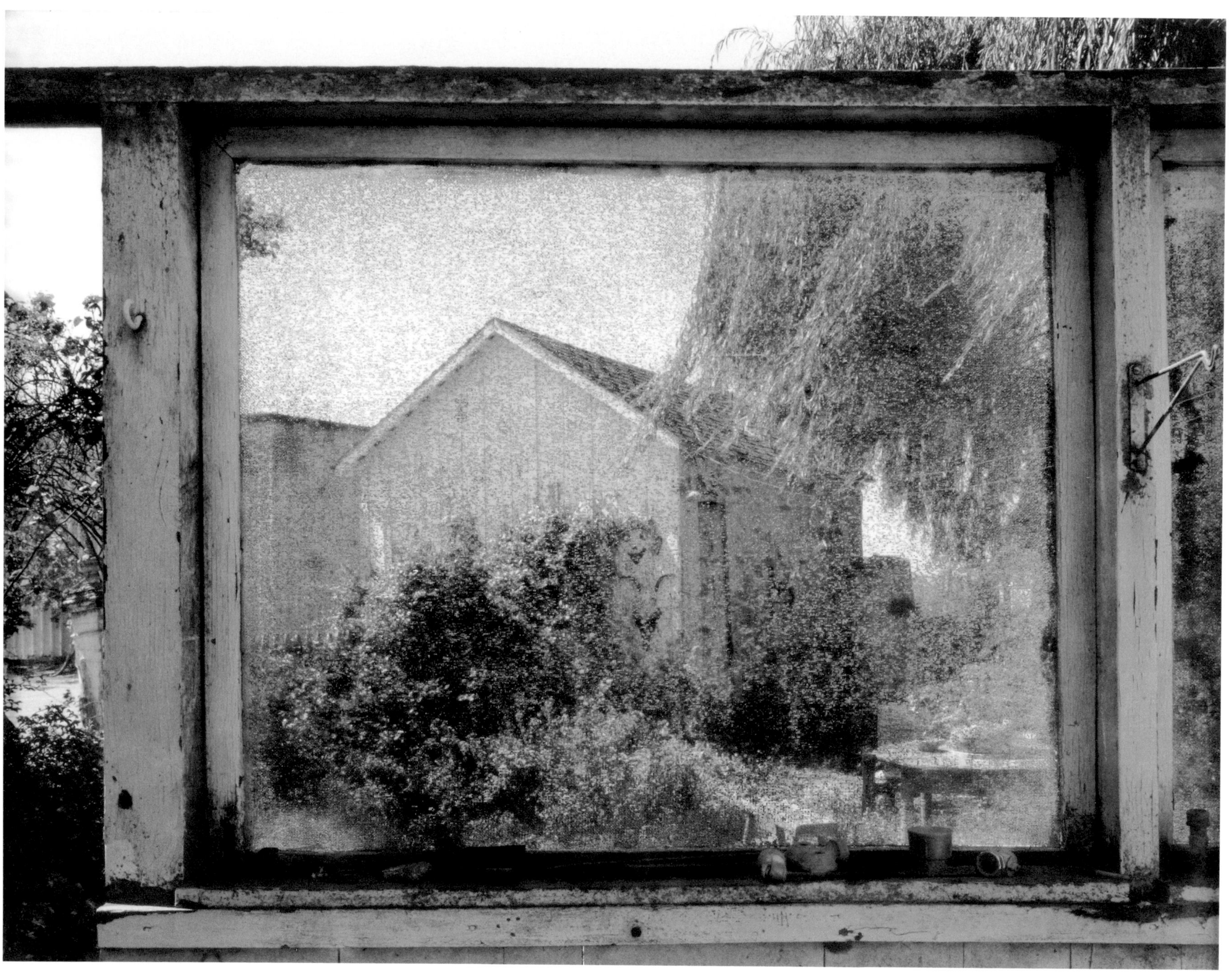

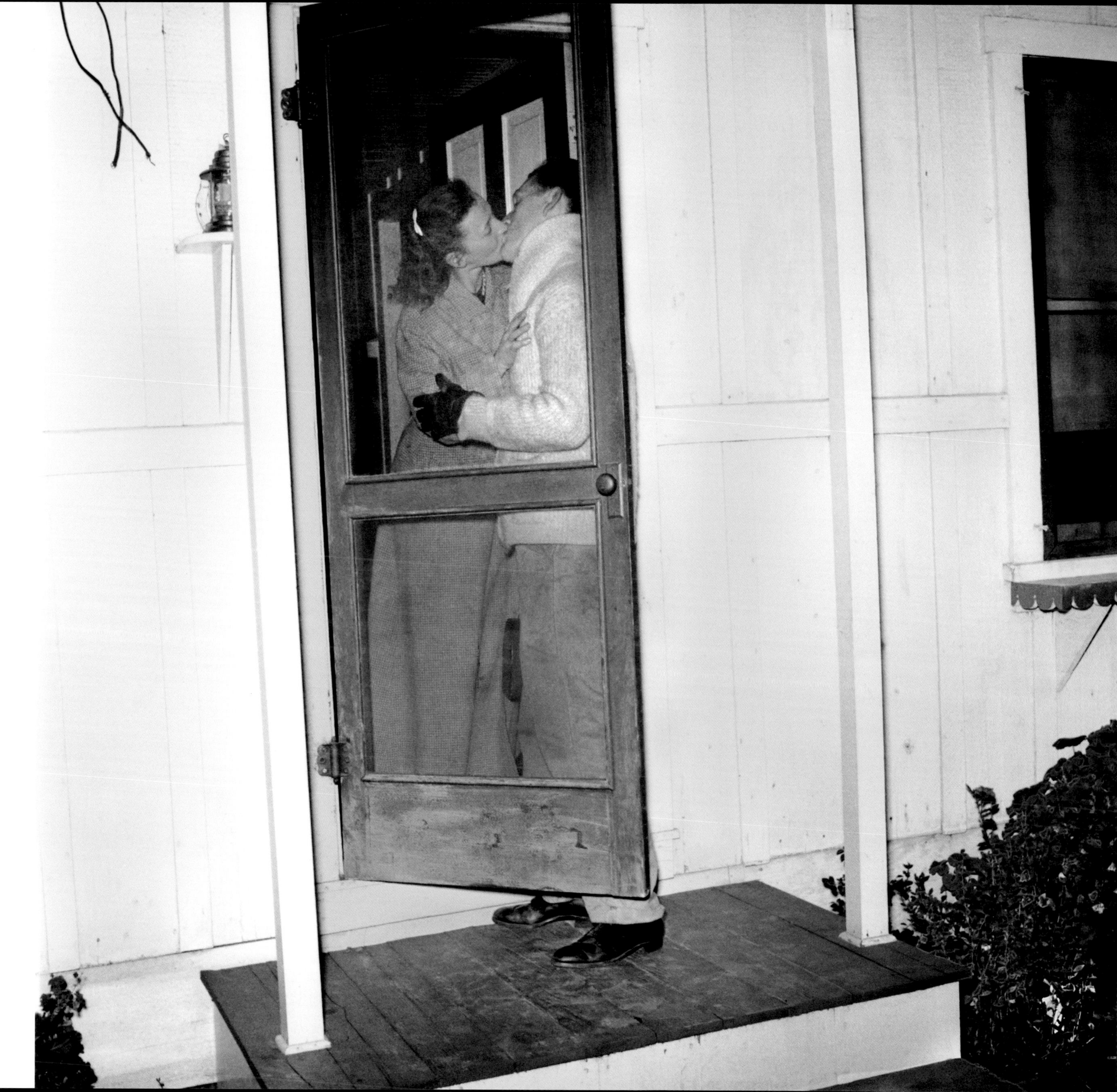

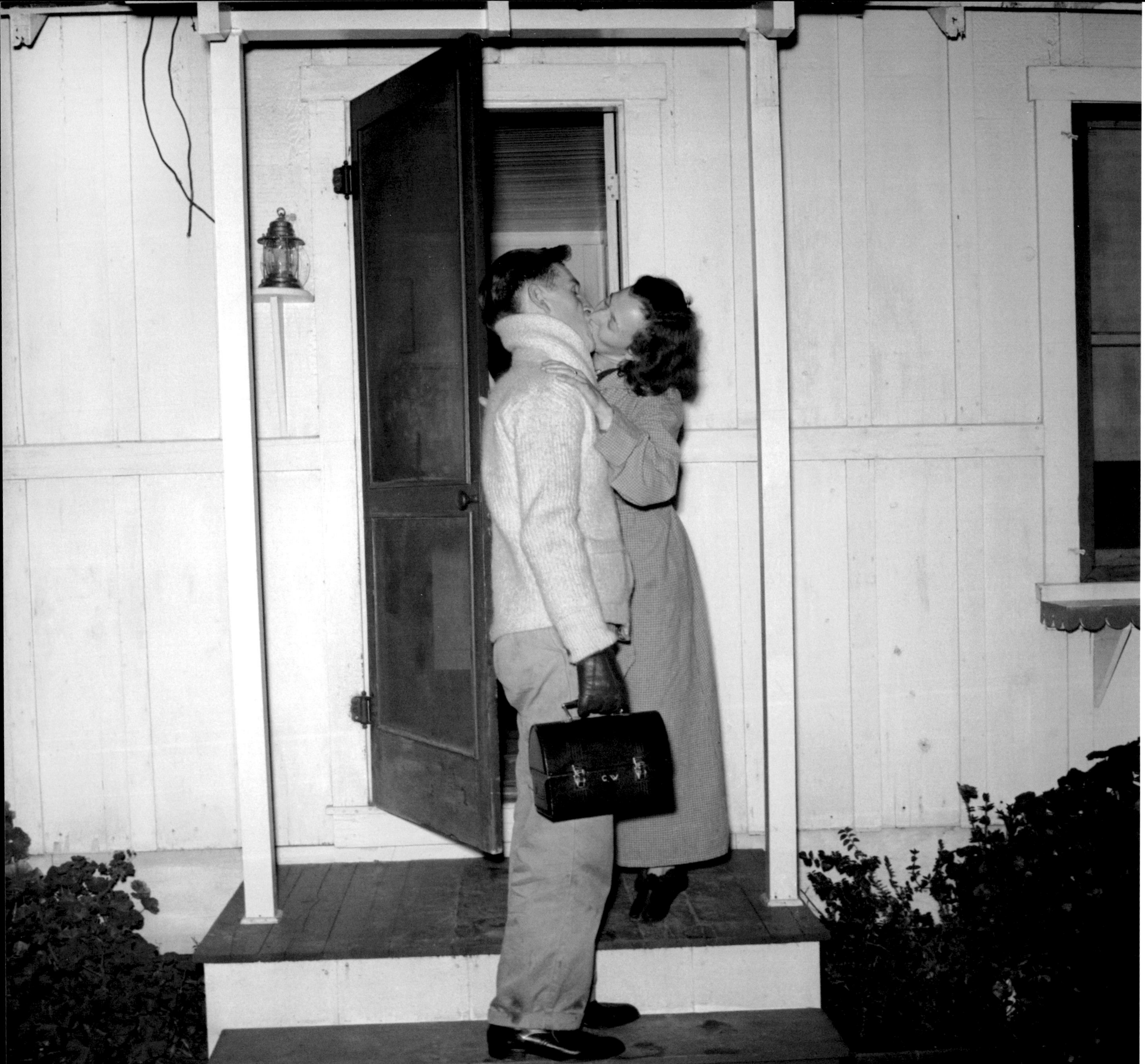

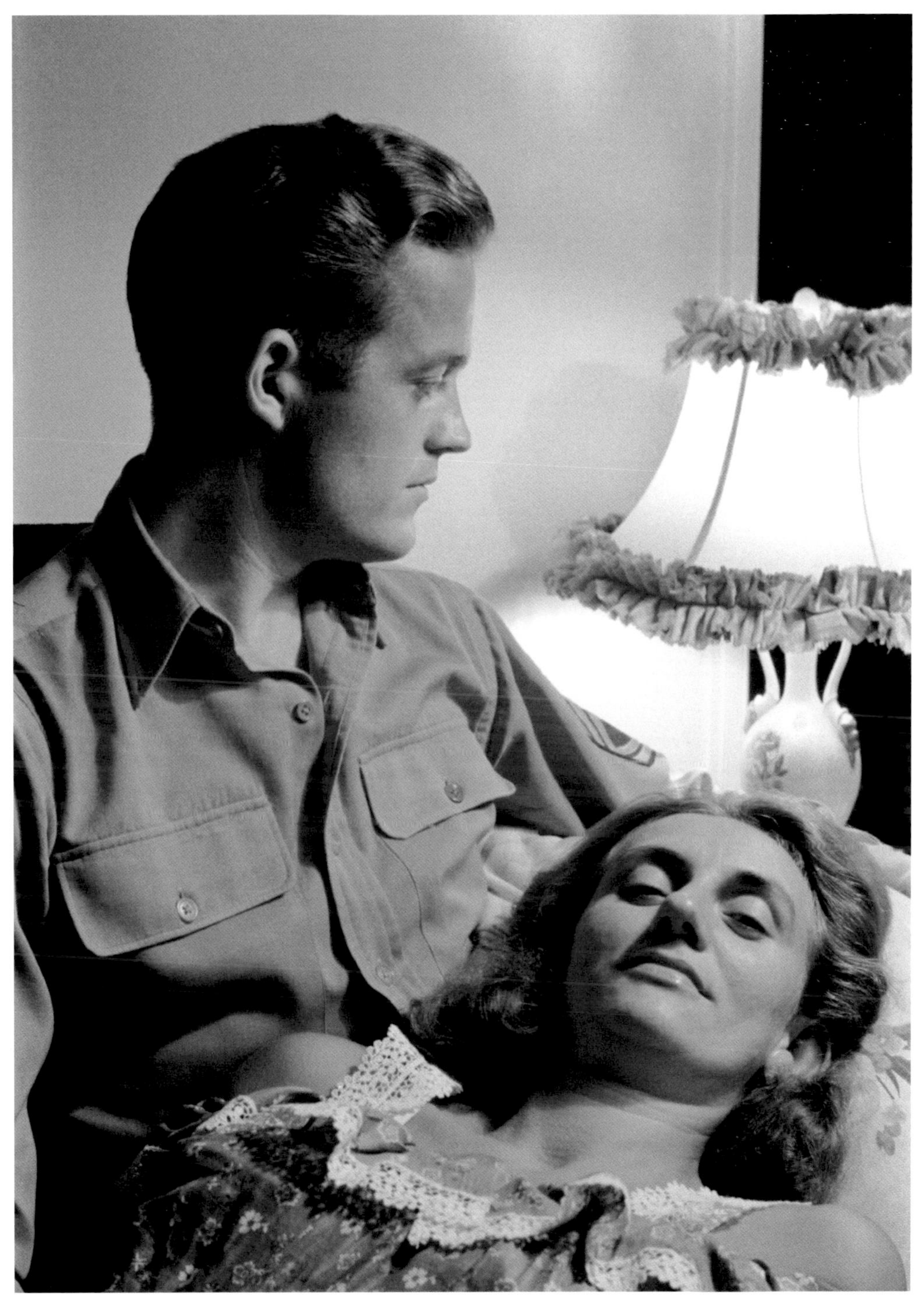

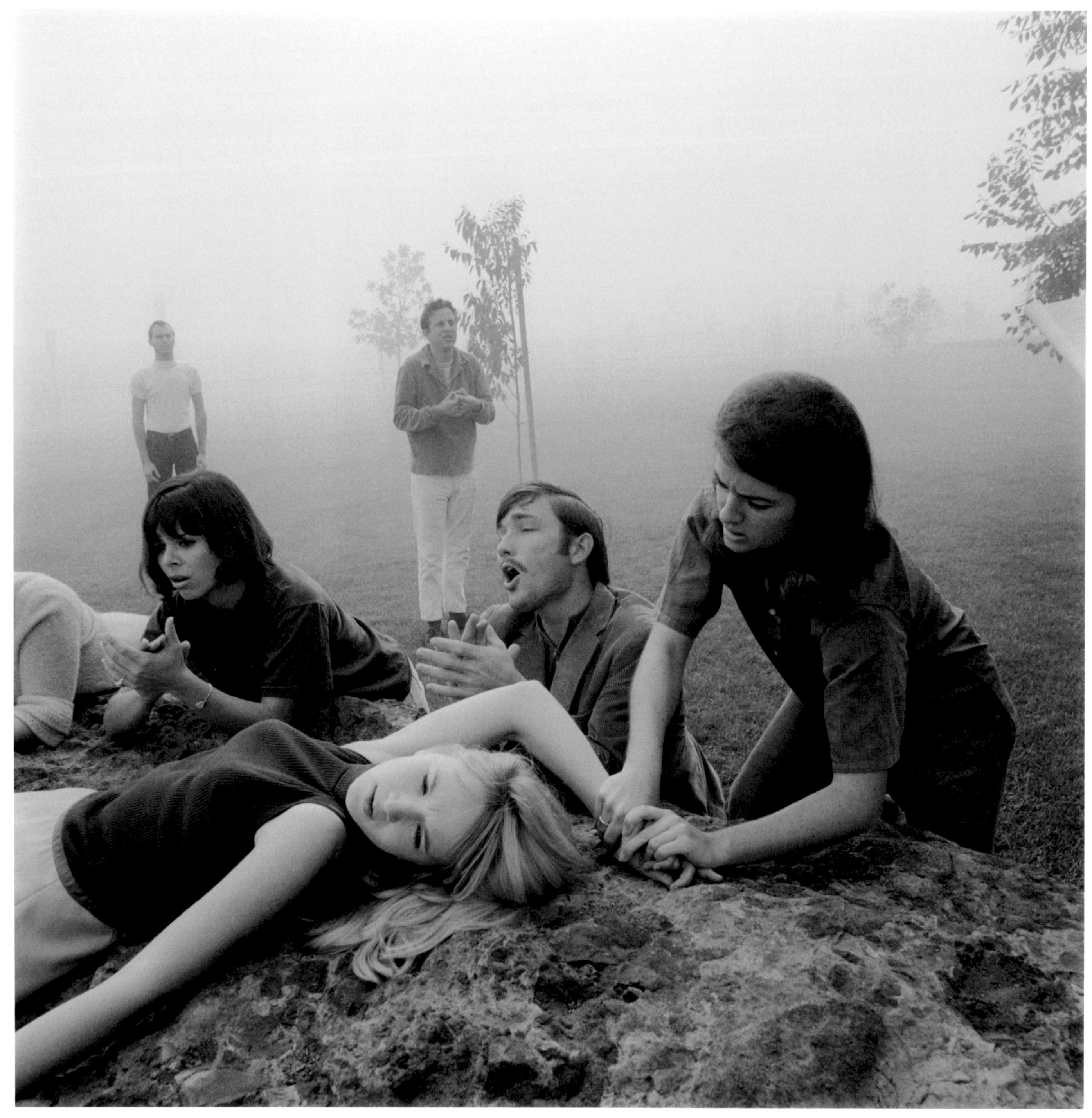

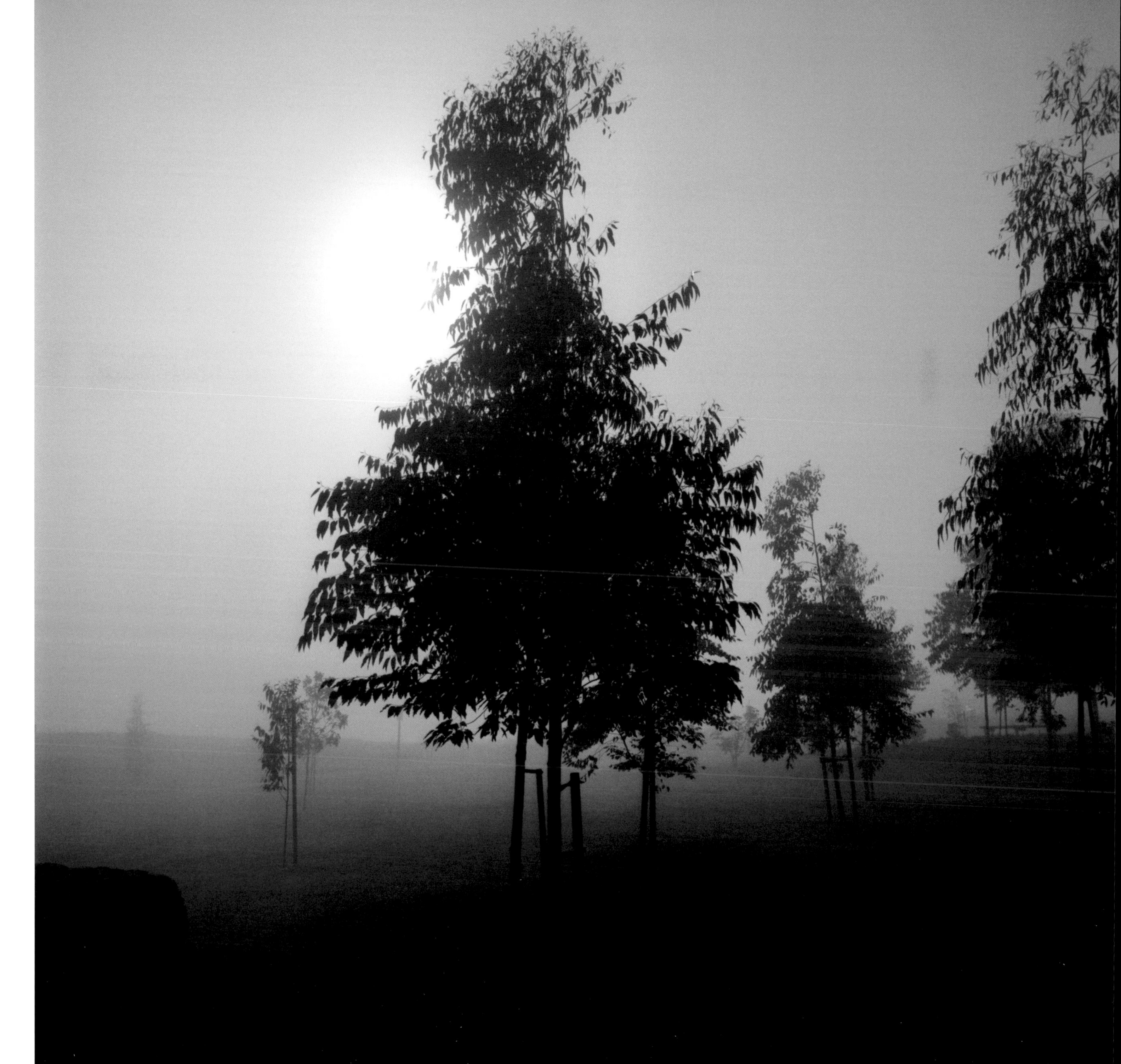

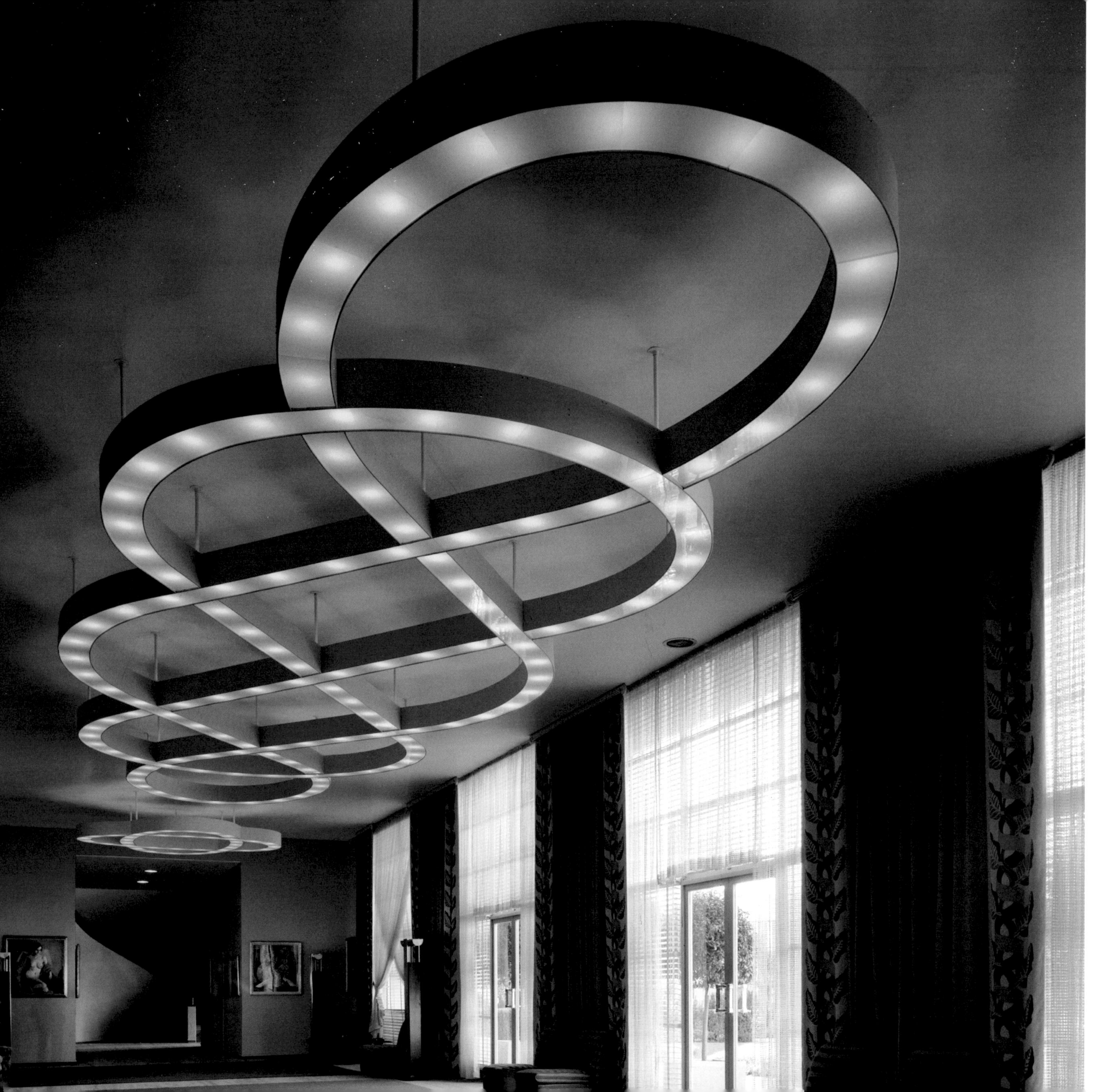

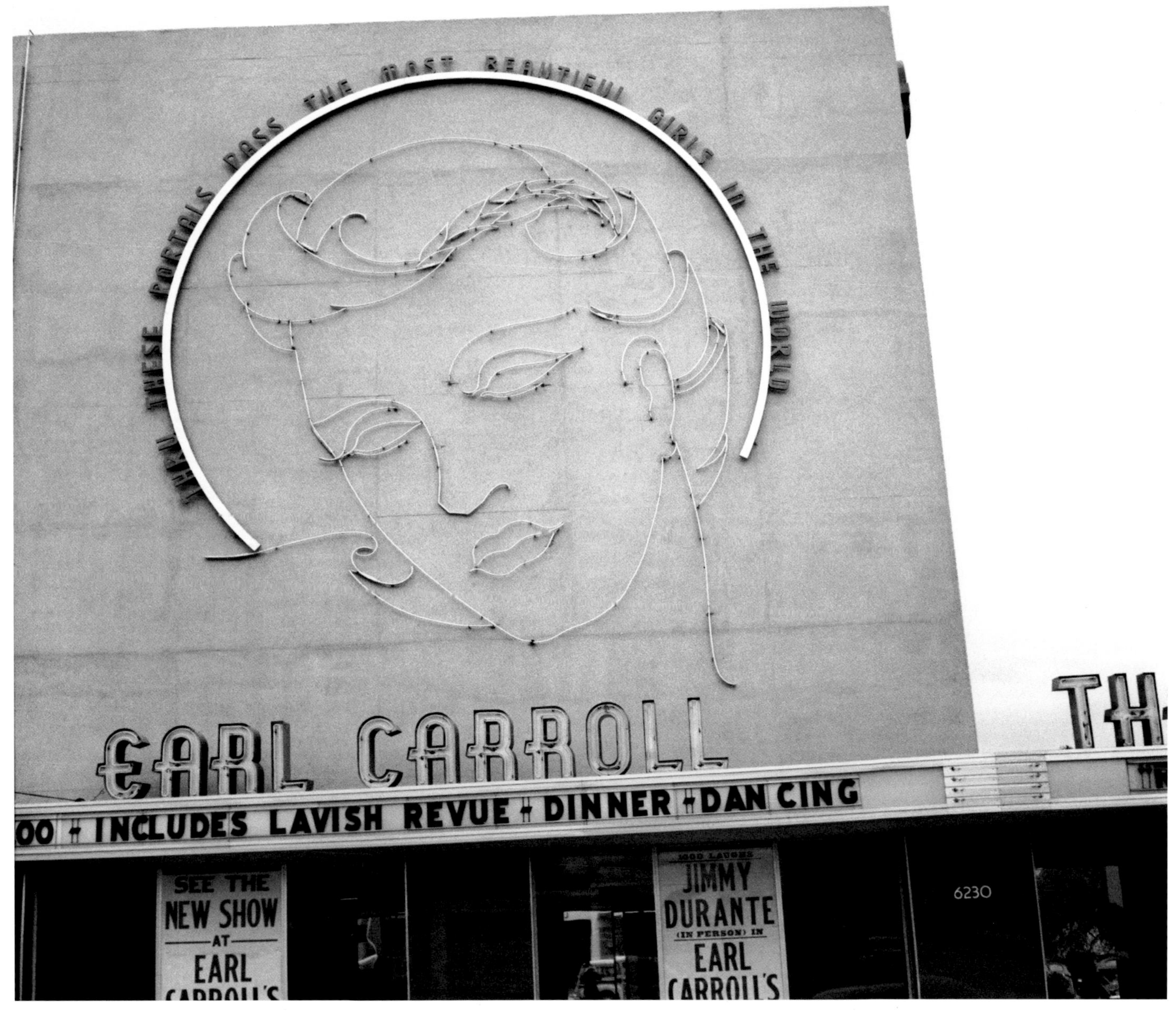
THRU THESE PORTALS PASS THE MOST BEAUTIFUL GIRLS IN THE WORLD
EARL CARROLL
TH-
00 * INCLUDES LAVISH REVUE * DINNER * DANCING
SEE THE
NEW SHOW
AT
EARL
CARROLL'S
1000 LAUGHS
JIMMY
DURANTE
(IN PERSON) IN
EARL
CARROLL'S
6230

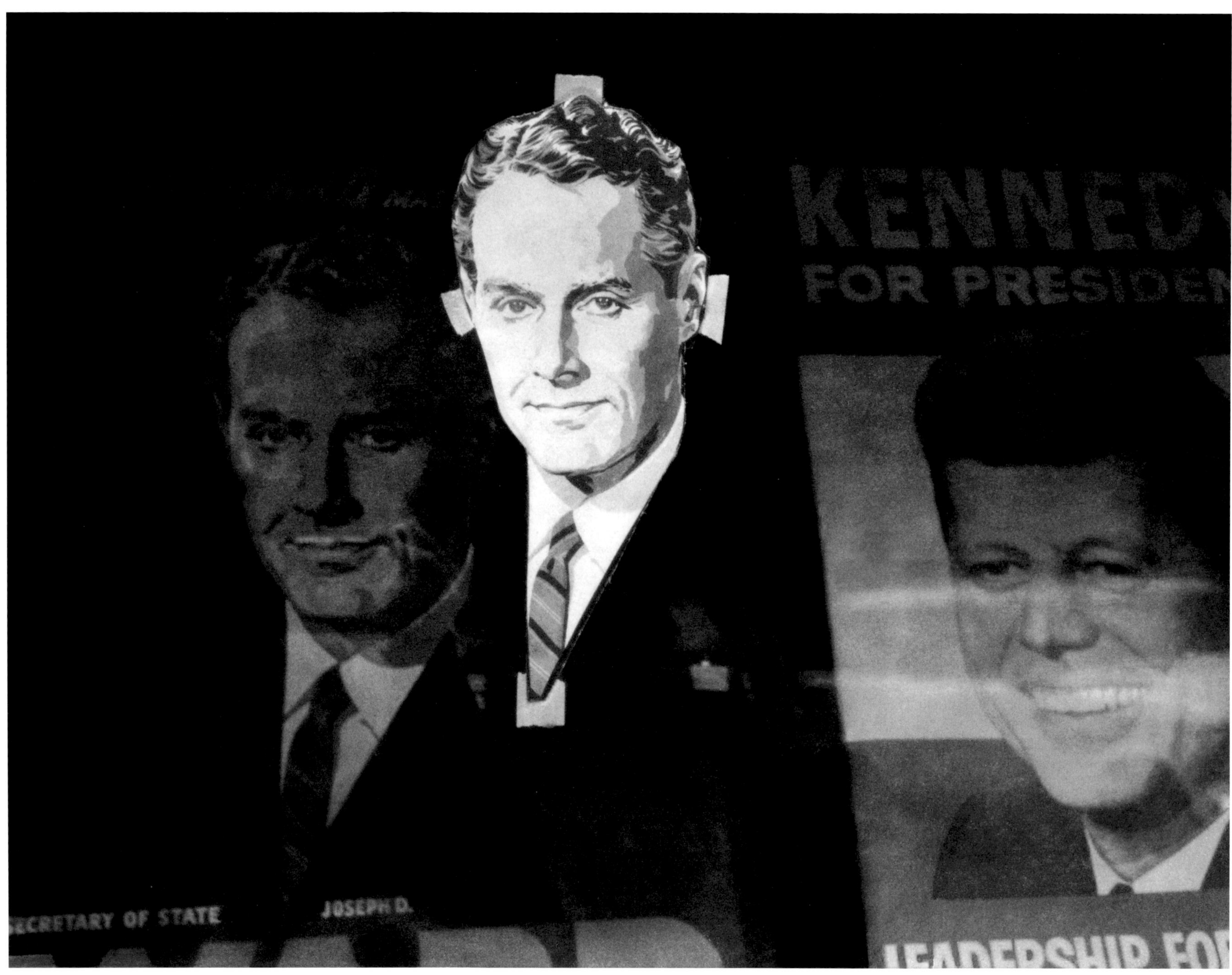
KENNED
FOR PRESIDEN
SECRETARY OF STATE
JOSEPH D.
LEADERSHIP FOR

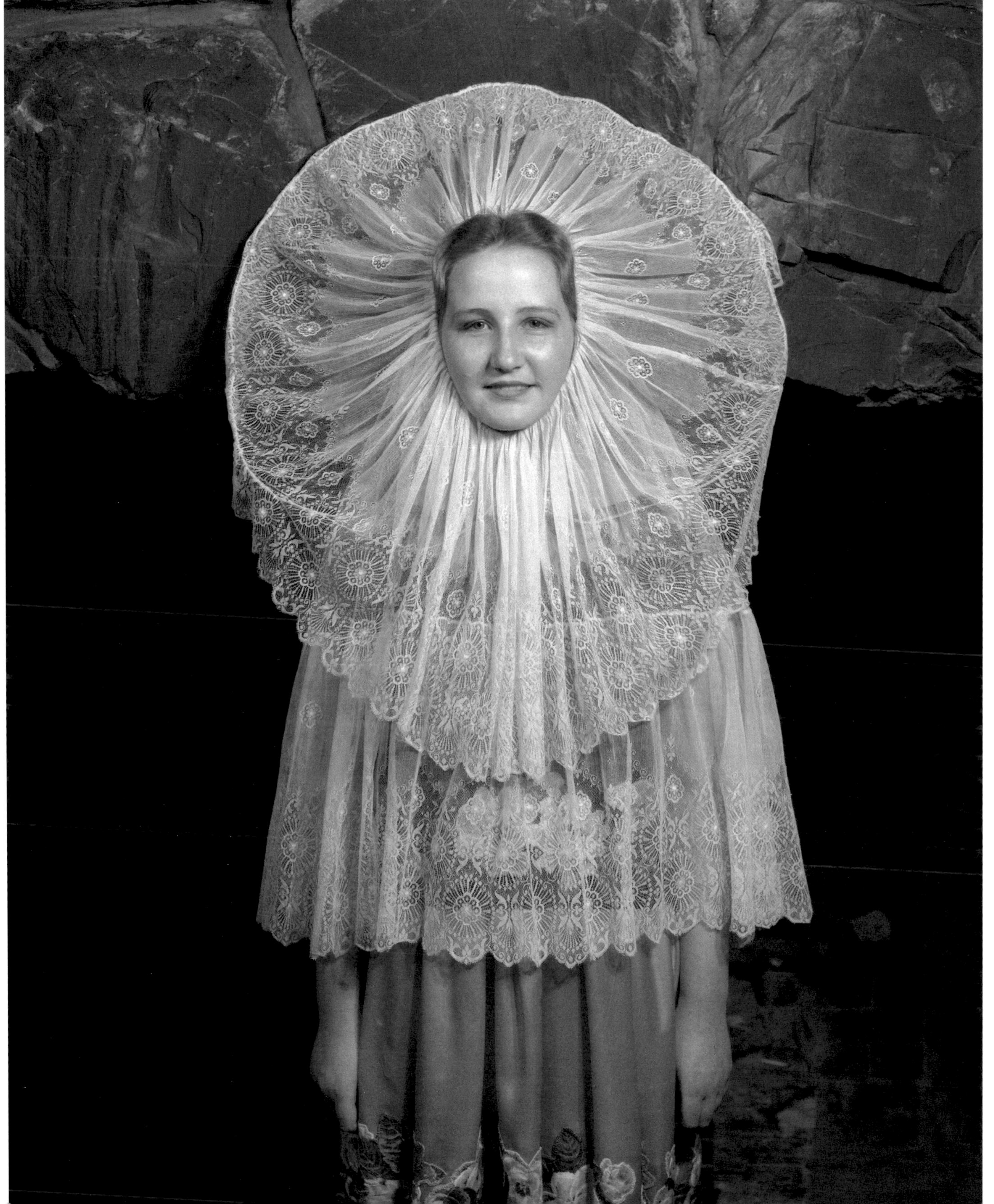

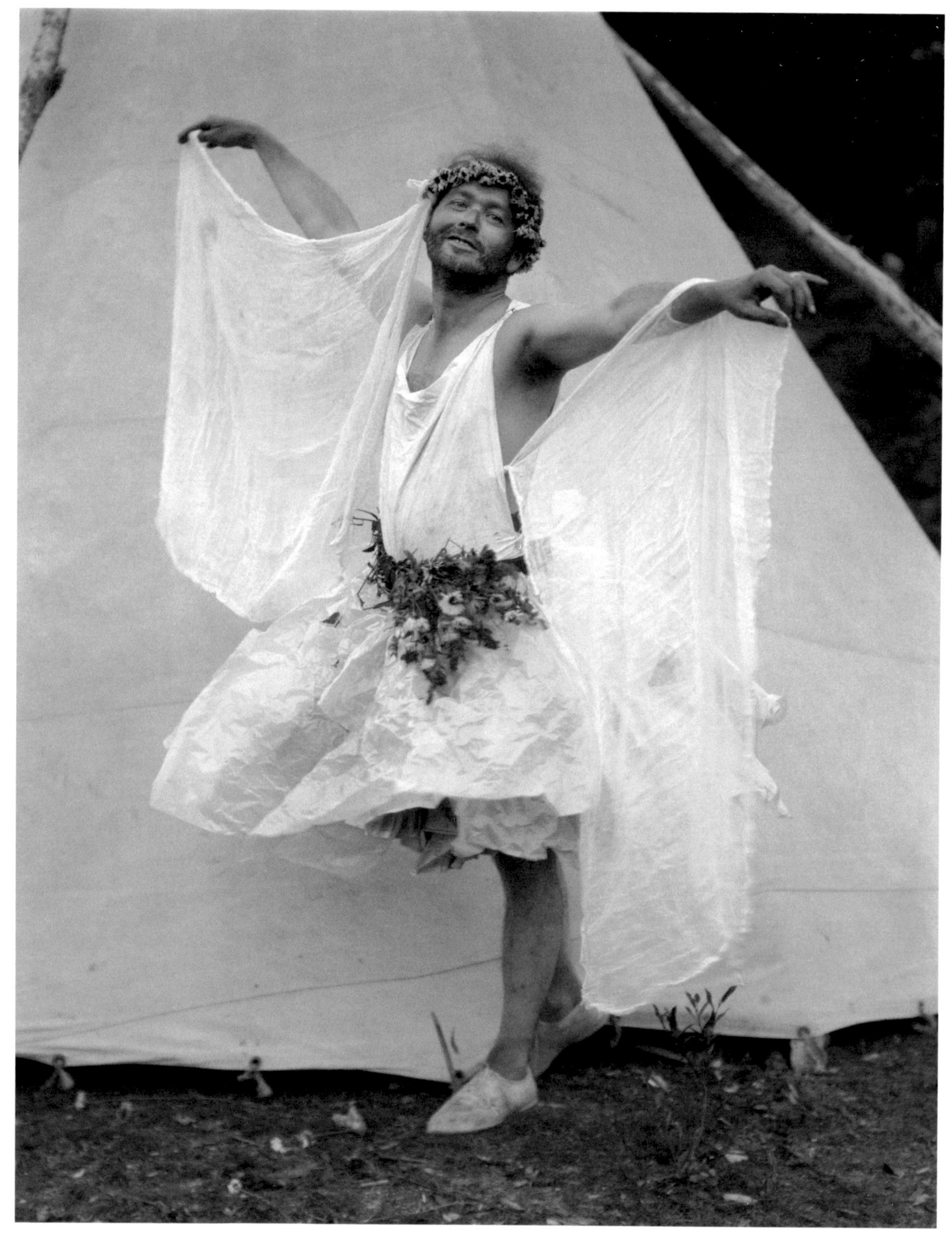

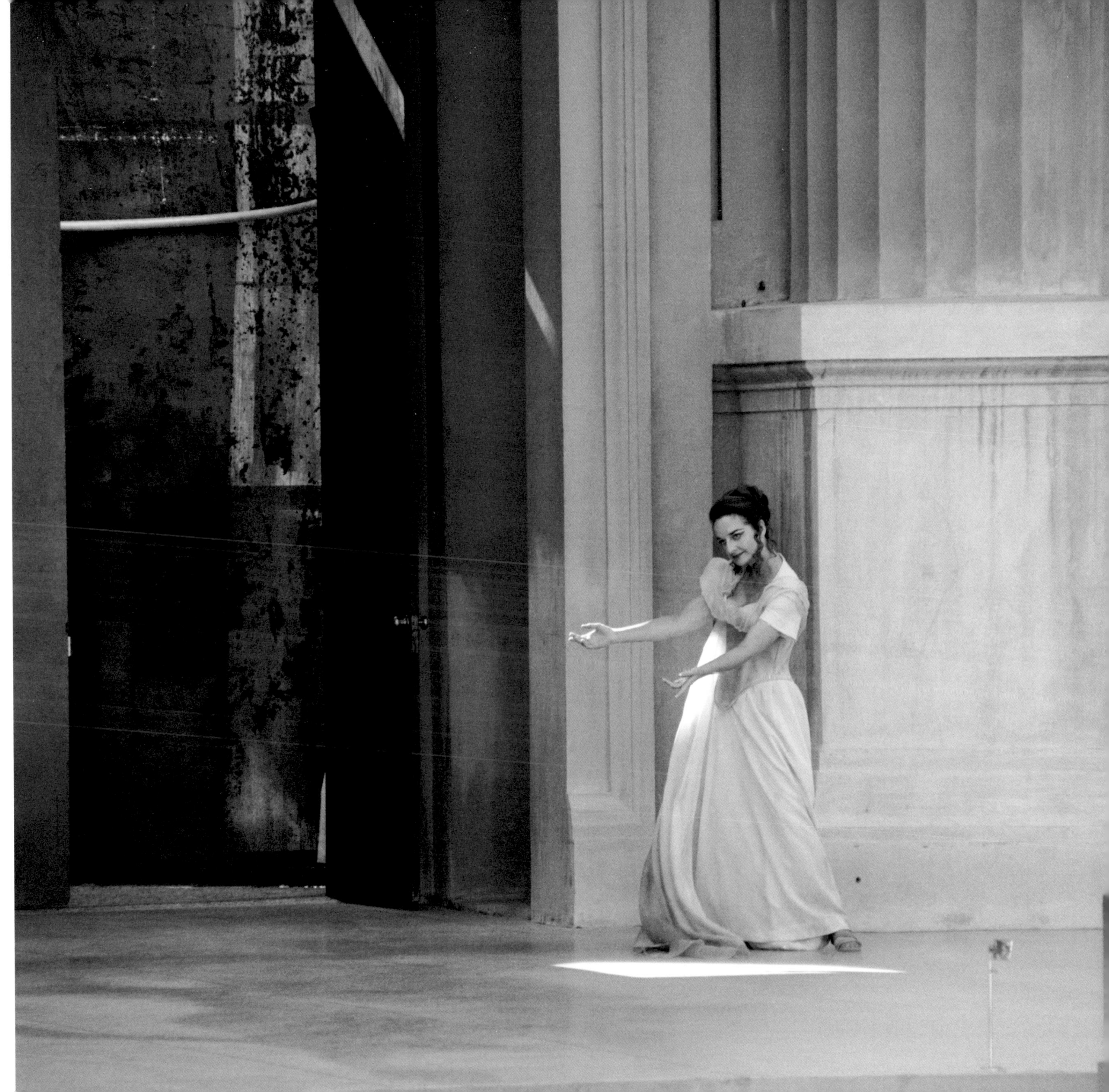

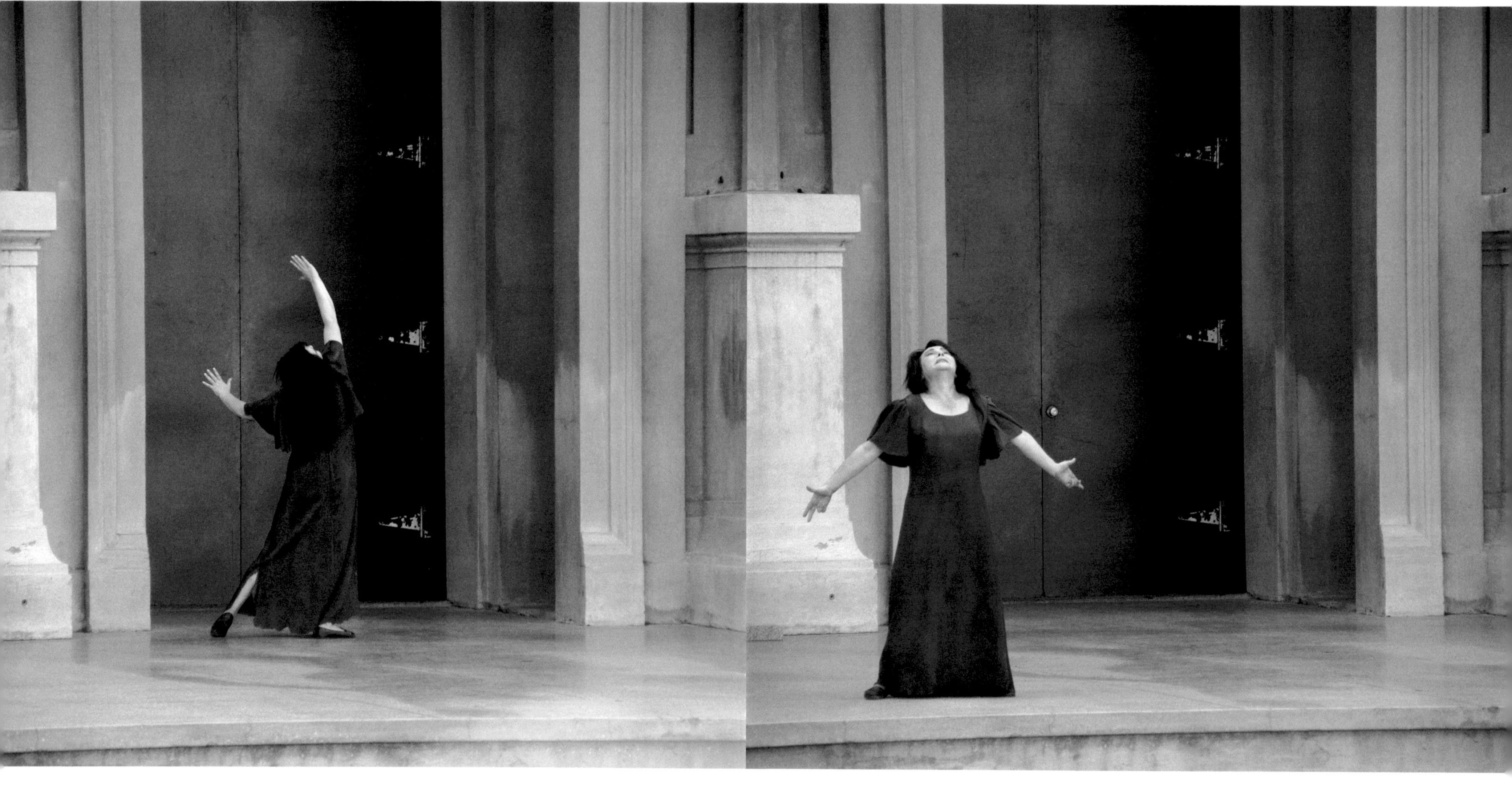

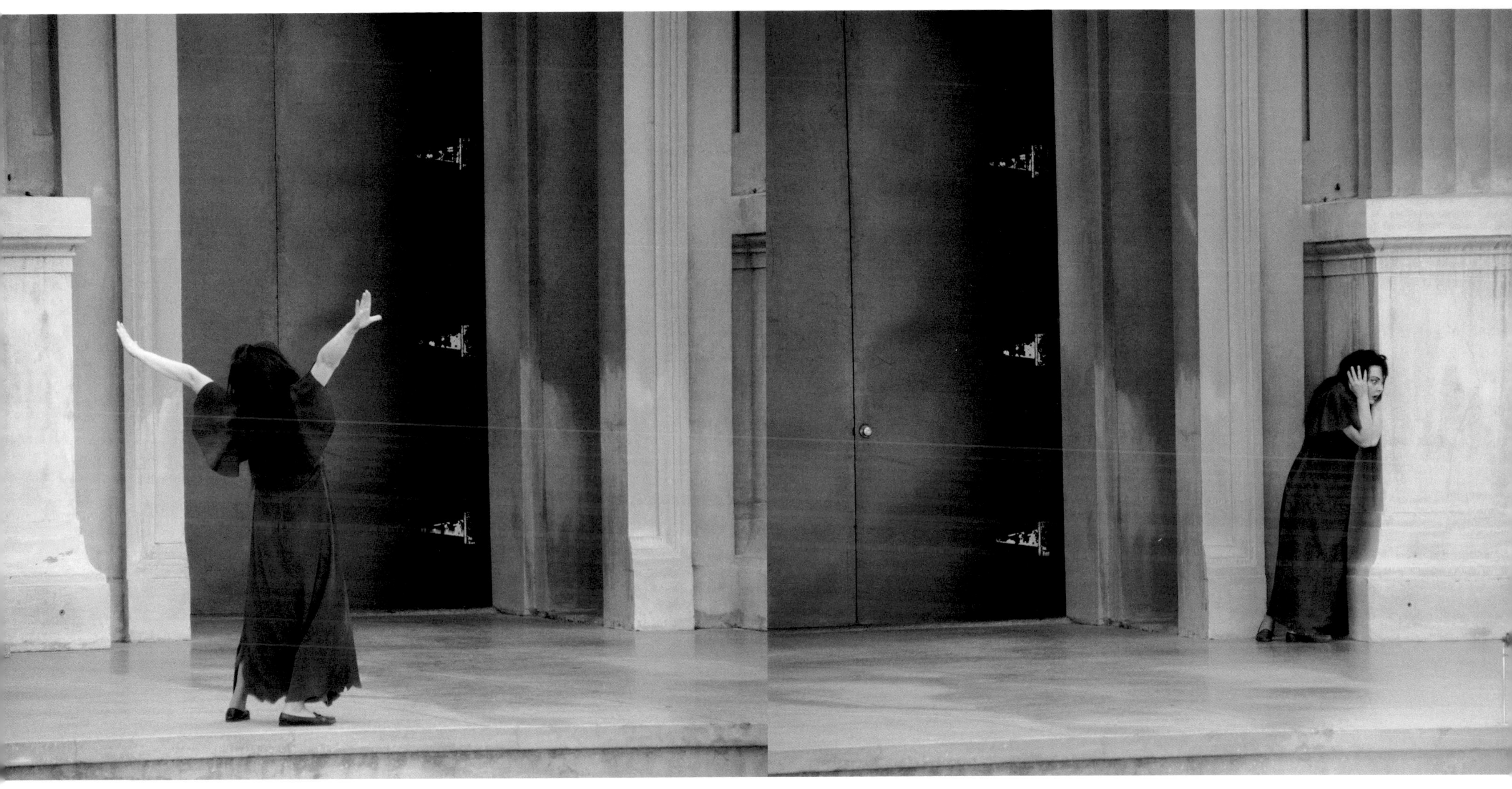

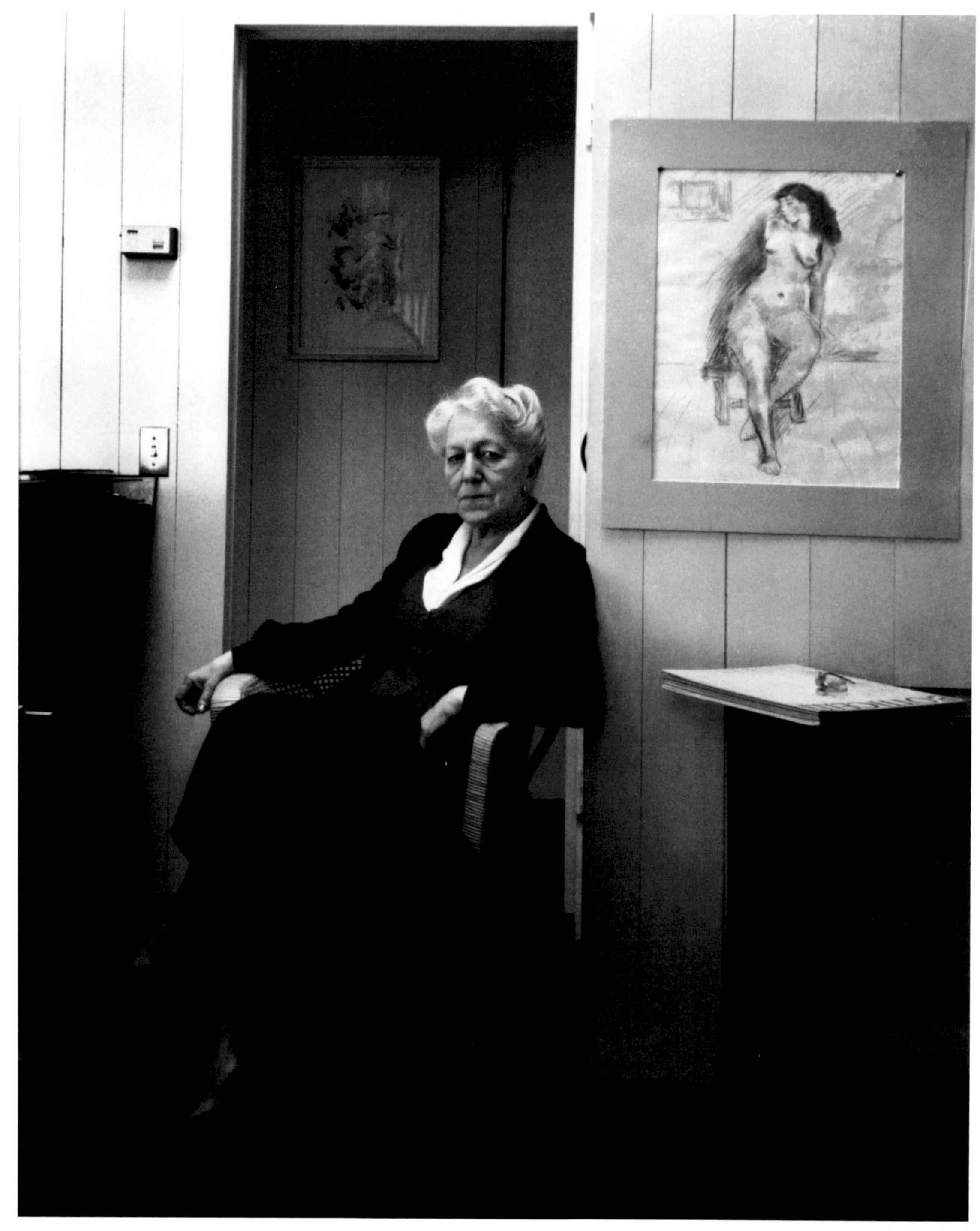

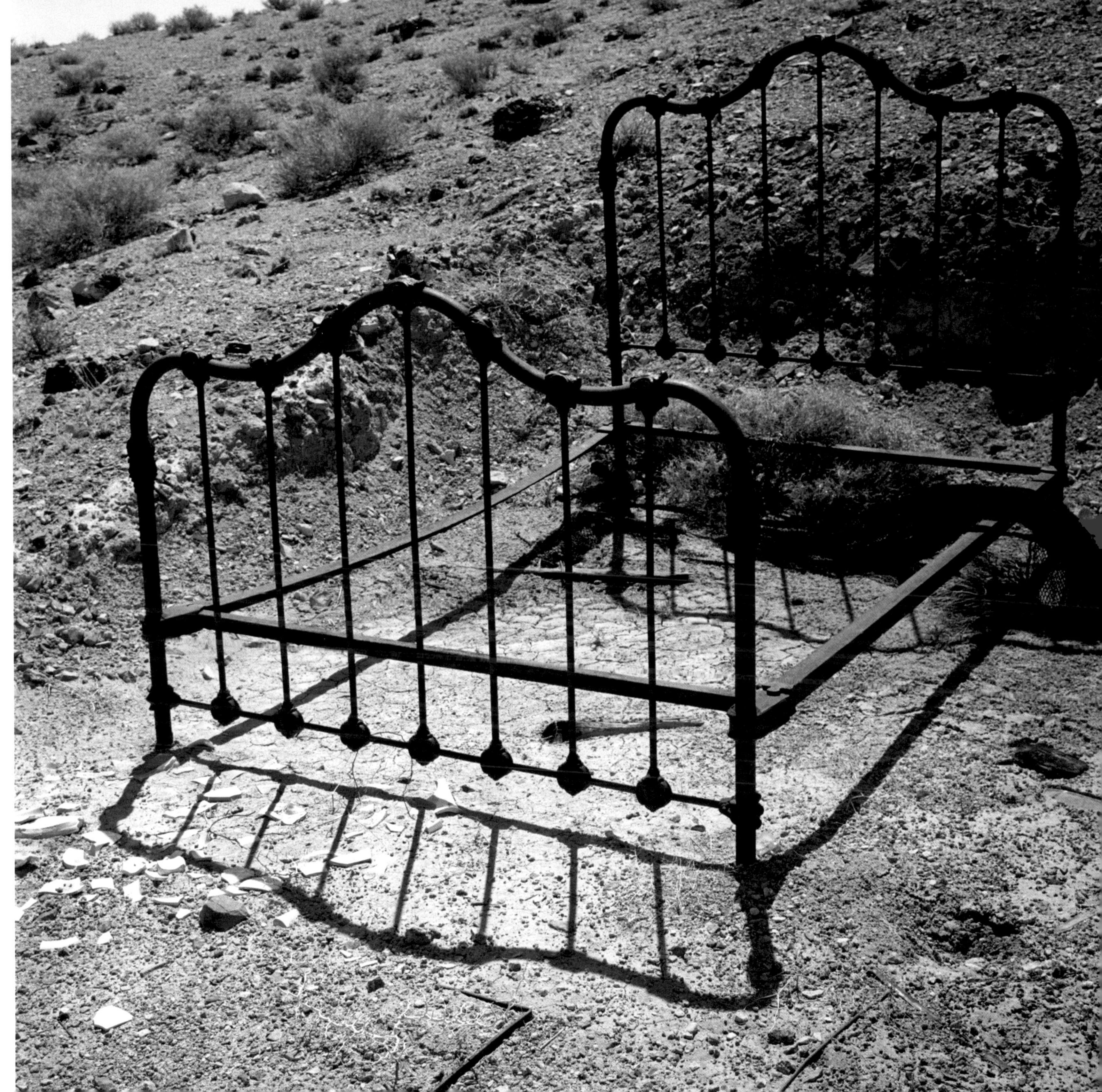

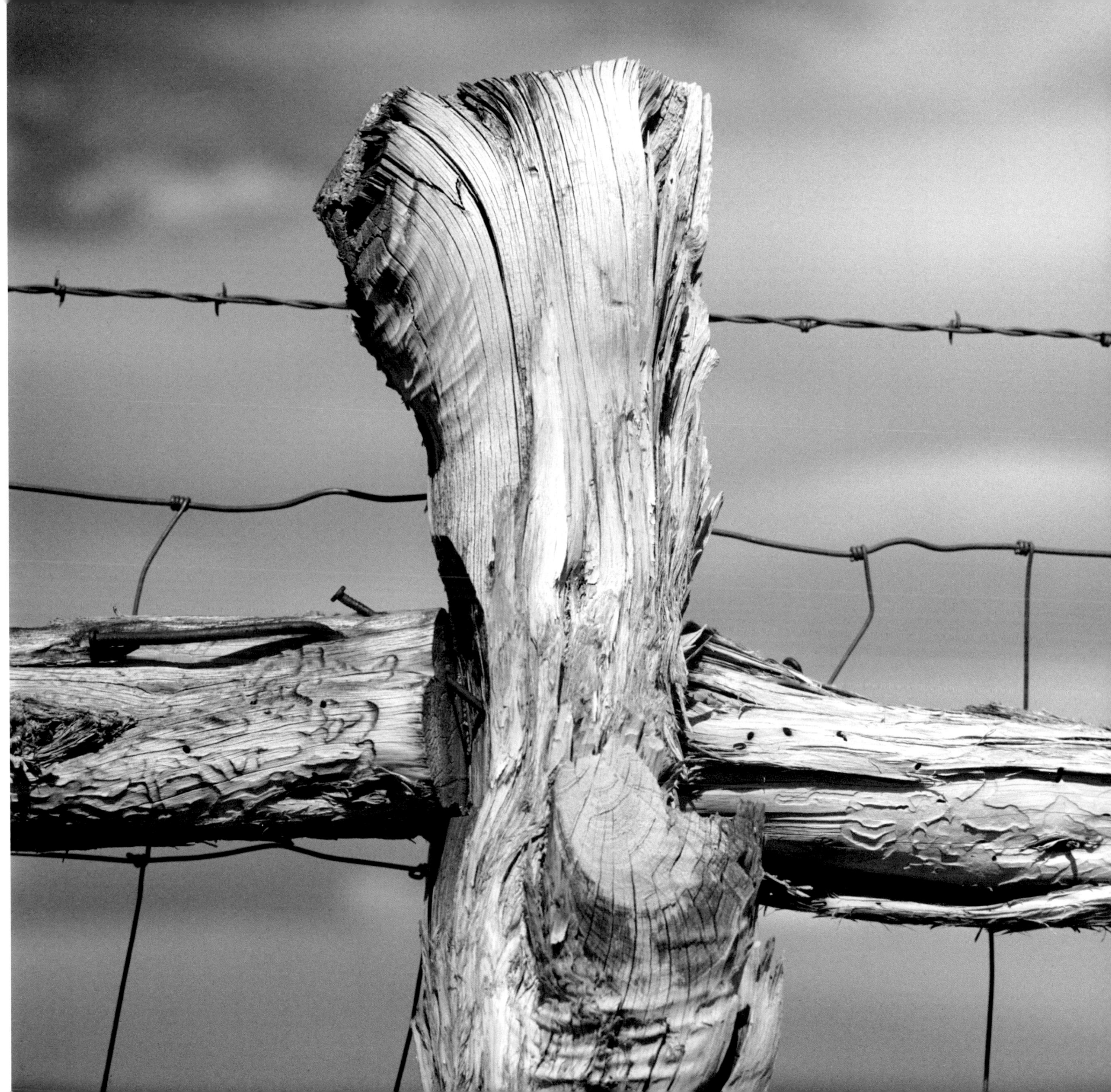

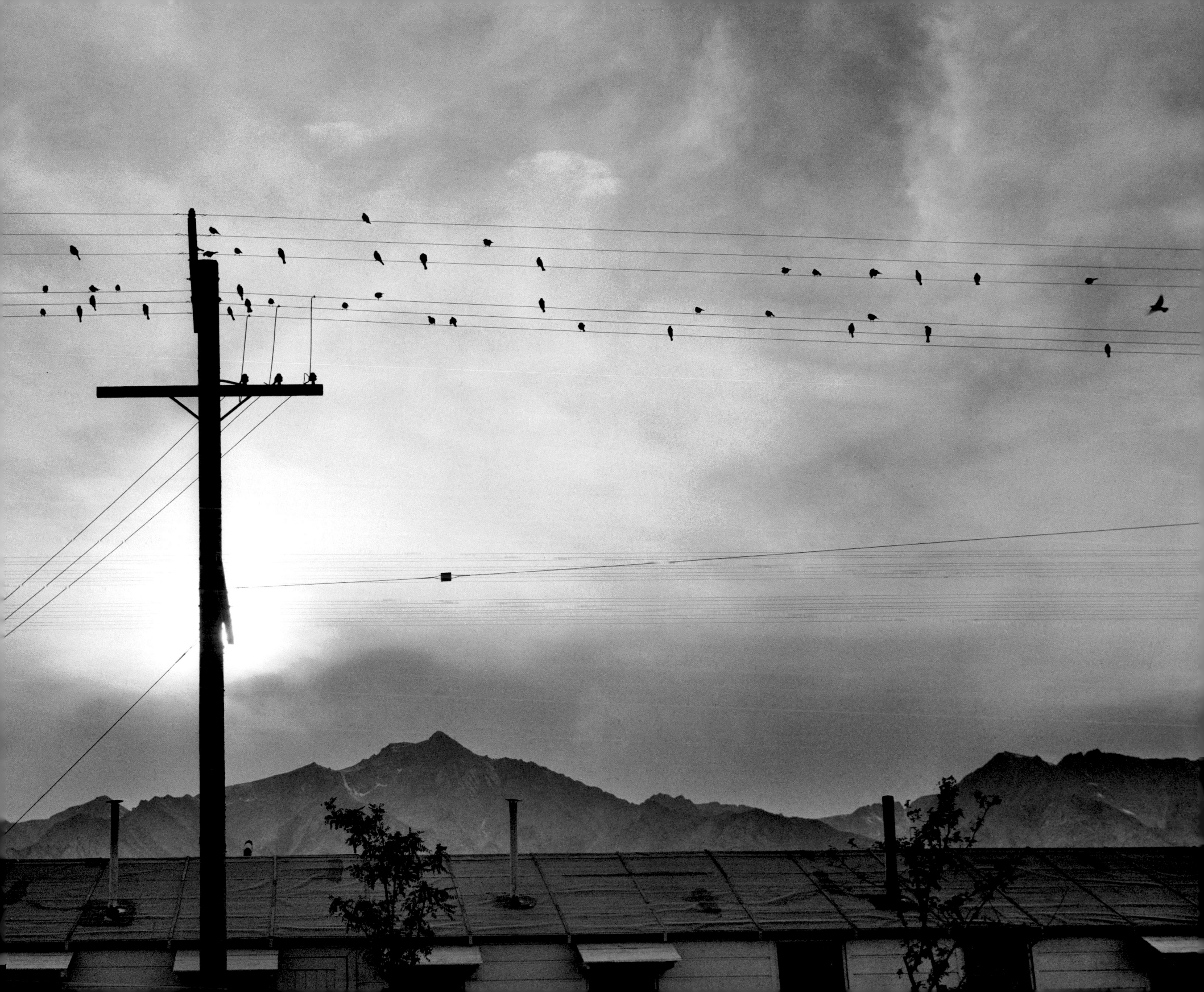

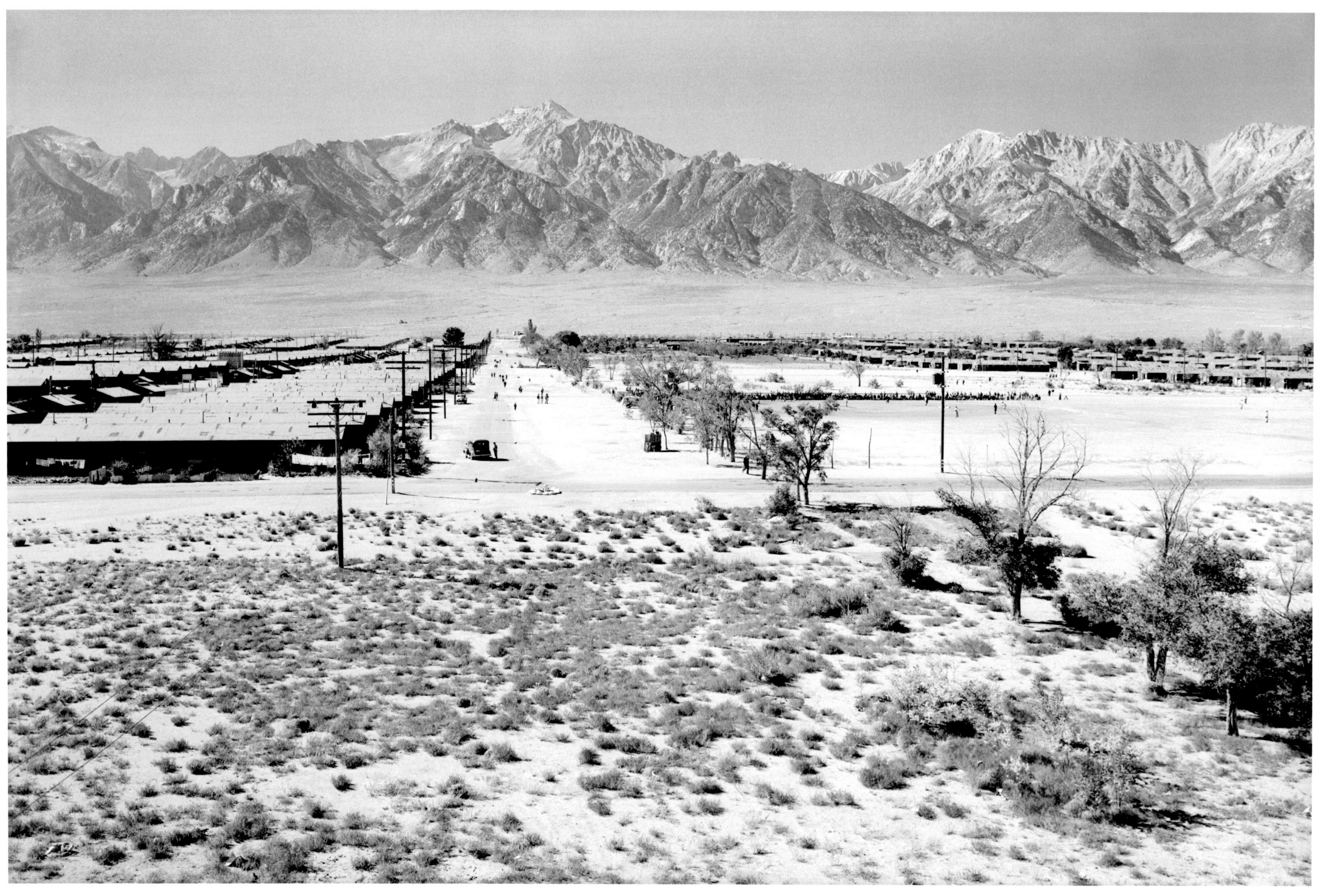

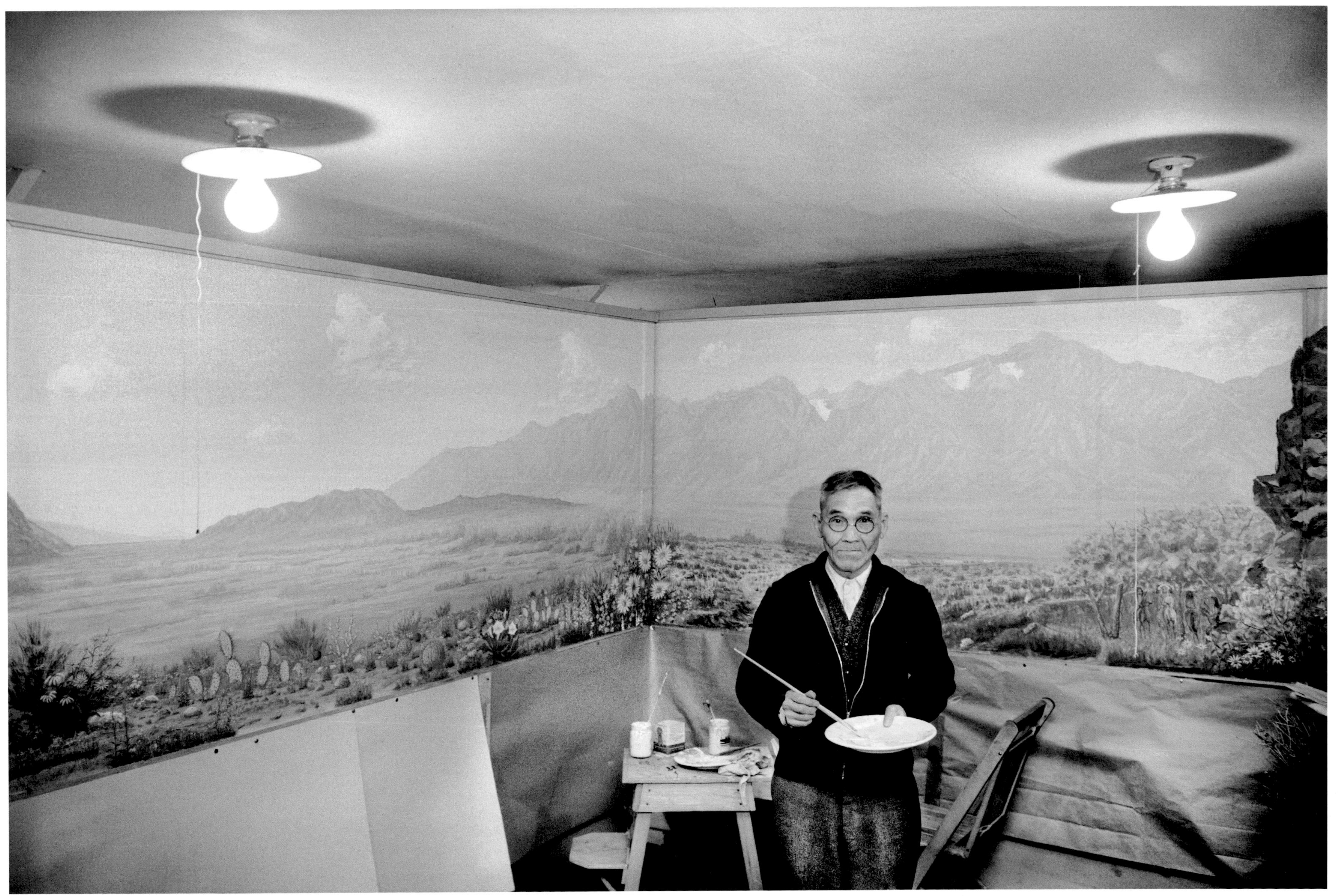

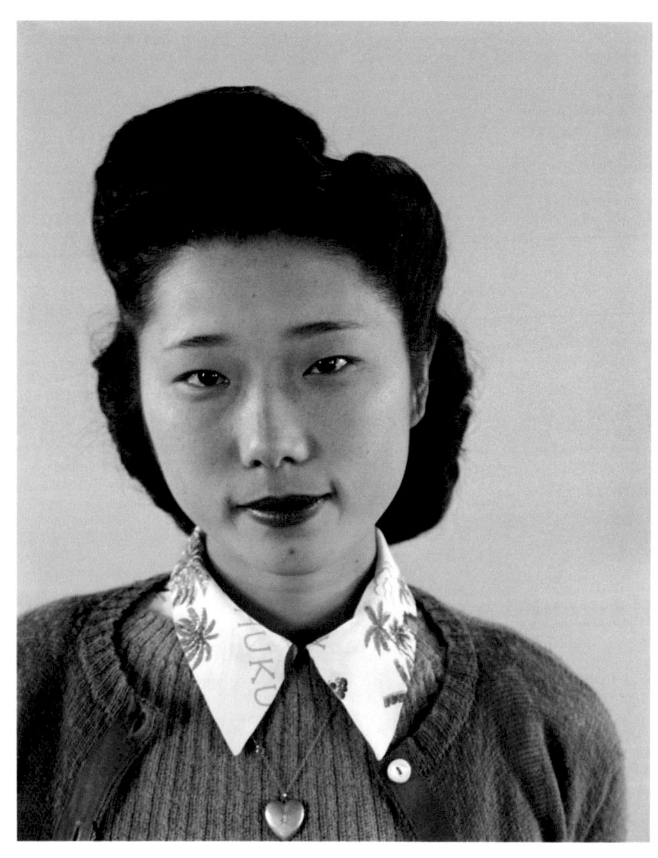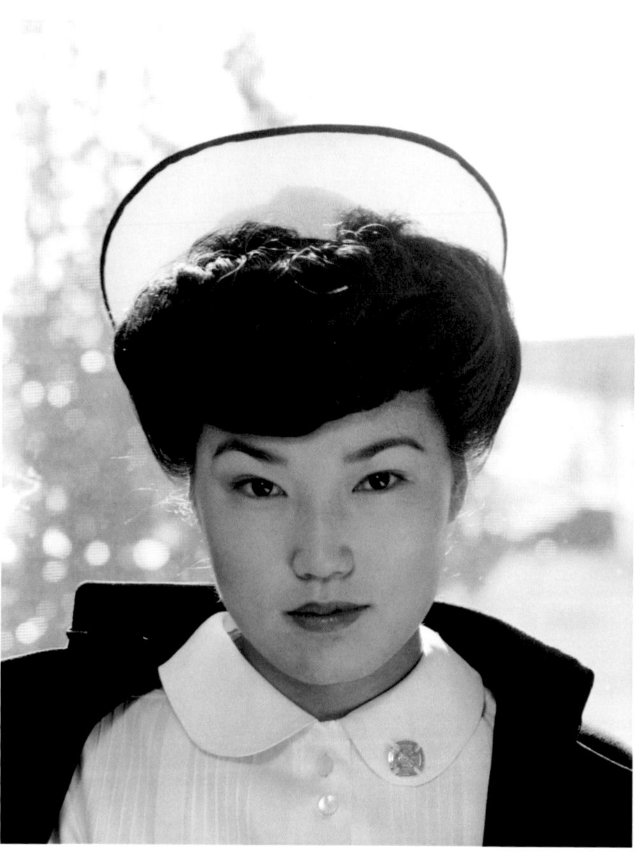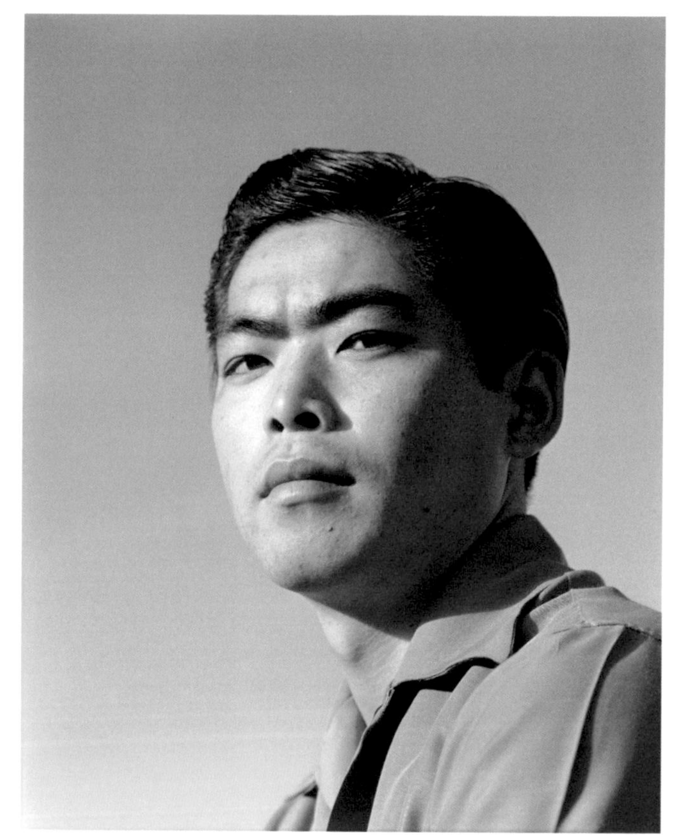

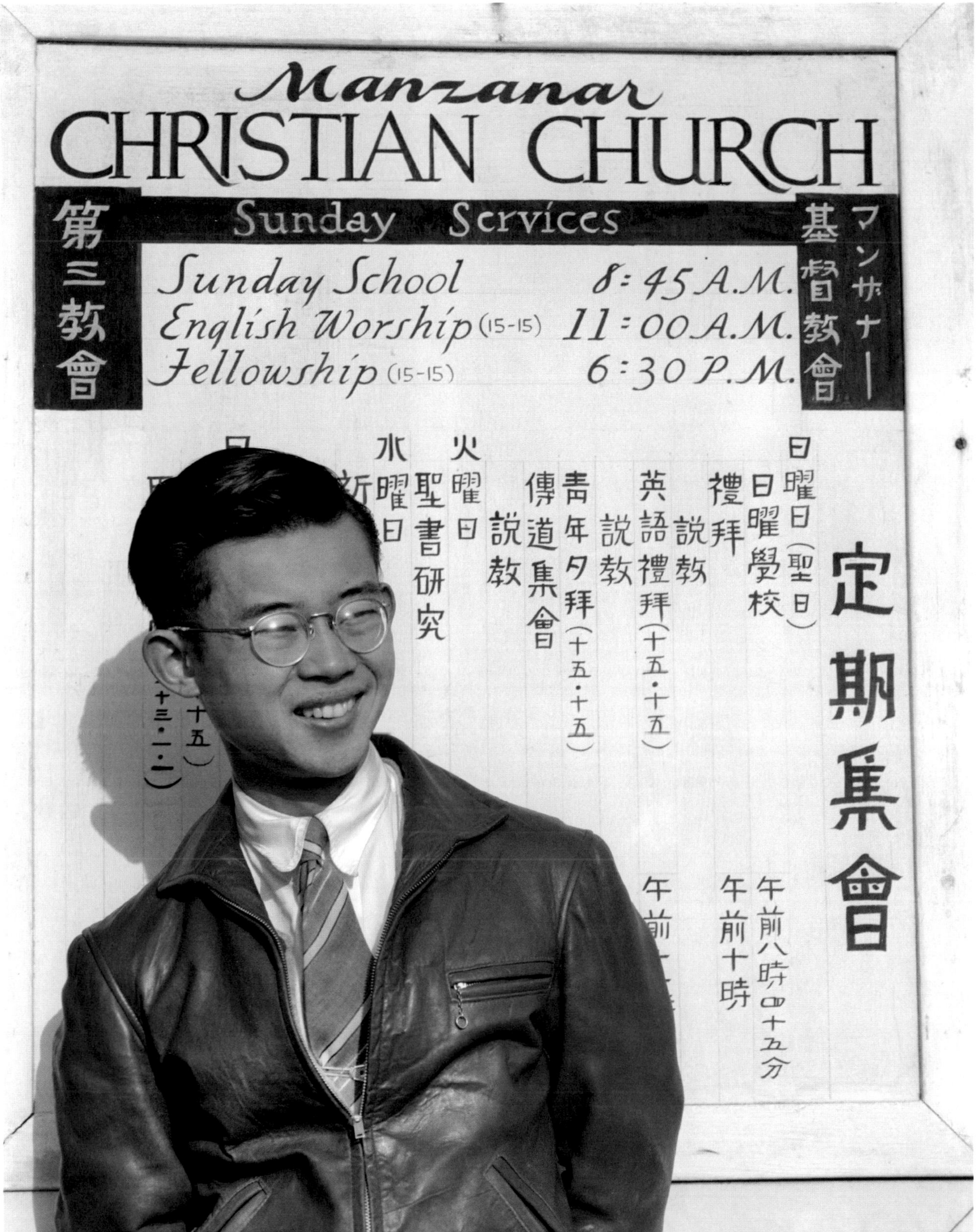

Manzanar
CHRISTIAN CHURCH
Sunday Services
第三教會
マンサナー
基督教會
Sunday School   8:45 A.M.
English Worship (15-15) 11:00 A.M.
Fellowship (15-15)   6:30 P.M.
定期集會
日曜日（聖日）
日曜學校
禮拜
説教
英語禮拜（十五・十五）
説教
青年夕拜（十五・十五）
傳道集會
説教
聖書研究
火曜日
水曜日
午前八時四十五分
午前十時

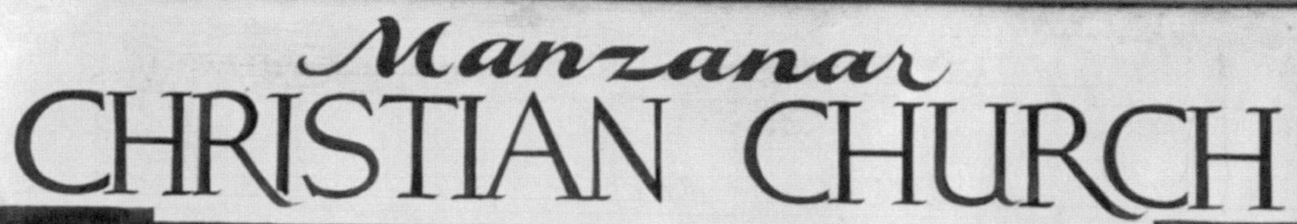

Manzanar
CHRISTIAN CHURCH
Sunday Services
第三教會
マンザナー
基督教會
Sunday School   8:45 A.M.
English Worship (15-15)   11:00 A.M.
Fellowship (15-15)   6:30 P.M.

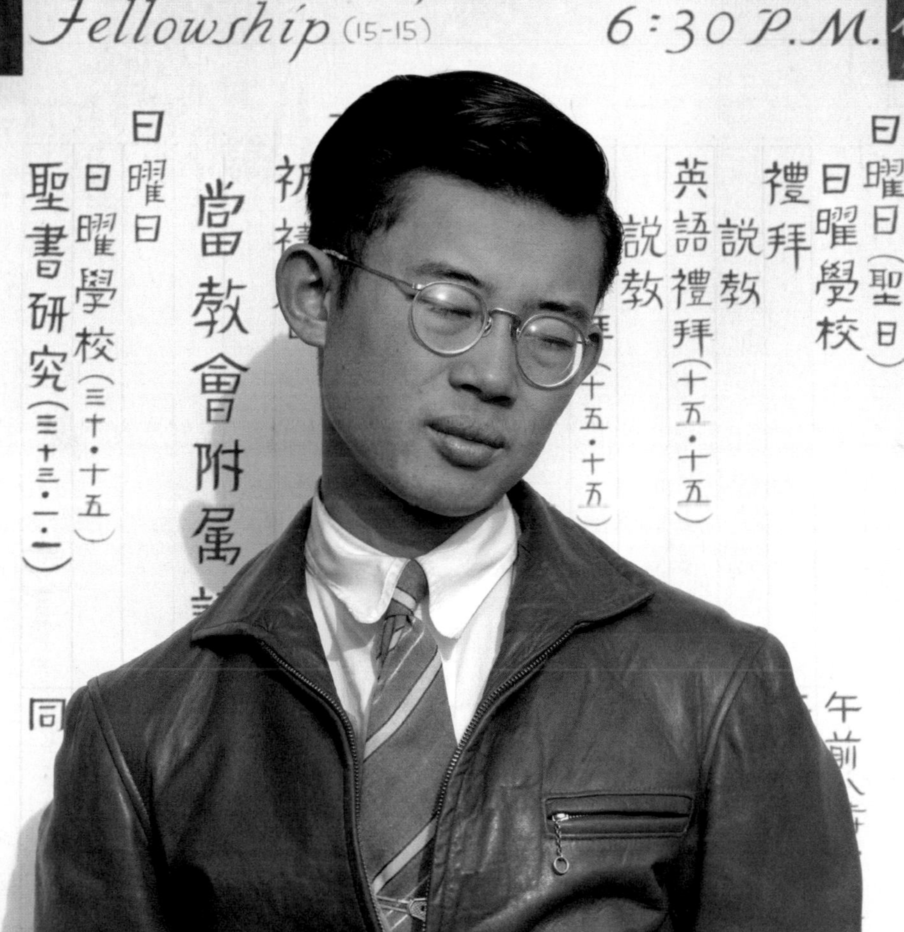

日曜日
日曜學校 (三〇・十五)
聖書研究 (三十三・一・二)
當教會附屬
同
日曜日 (聖日)
日曜學校
禮拜
英語禮拜 (十五・十五)
説教
定期集會

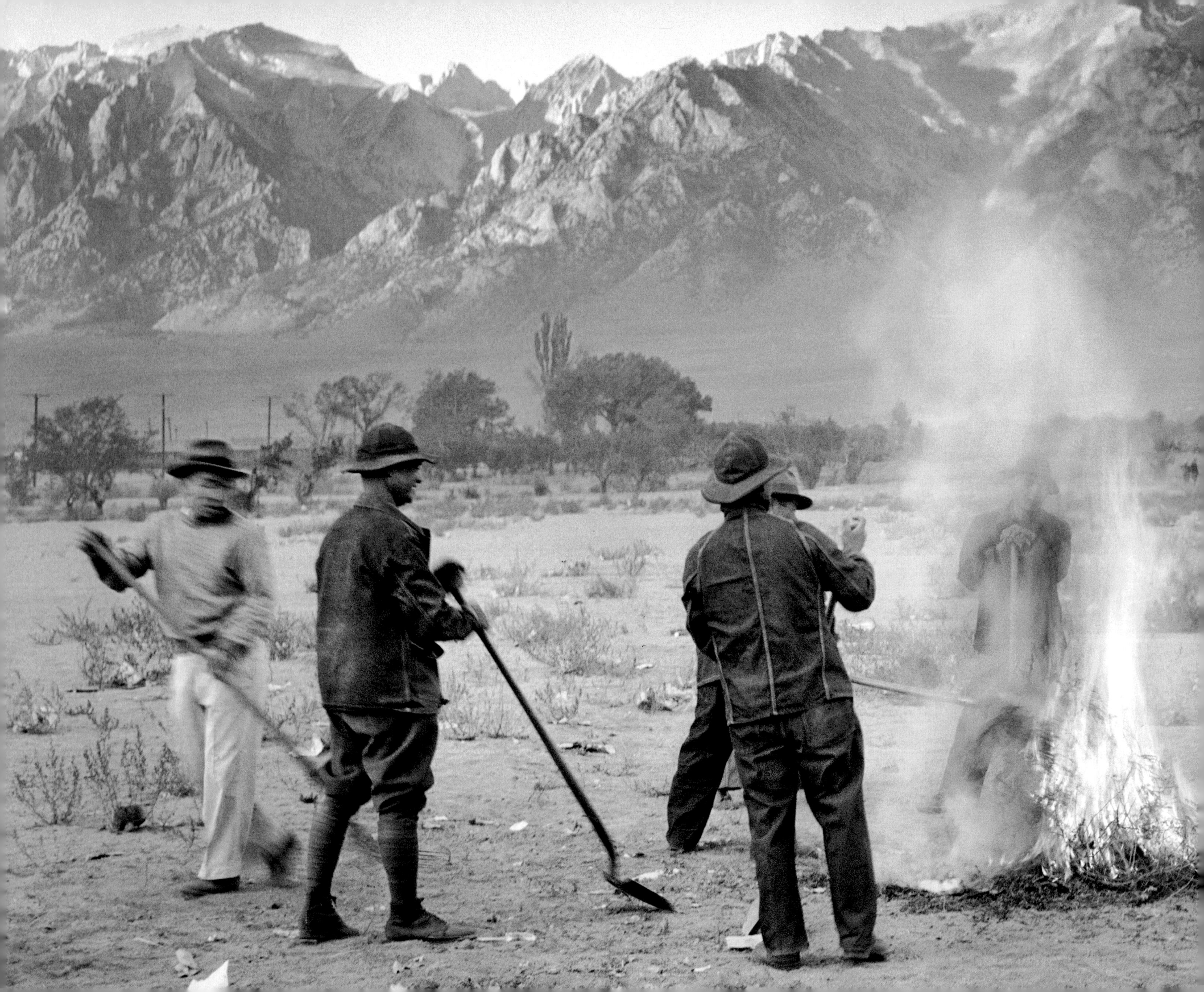

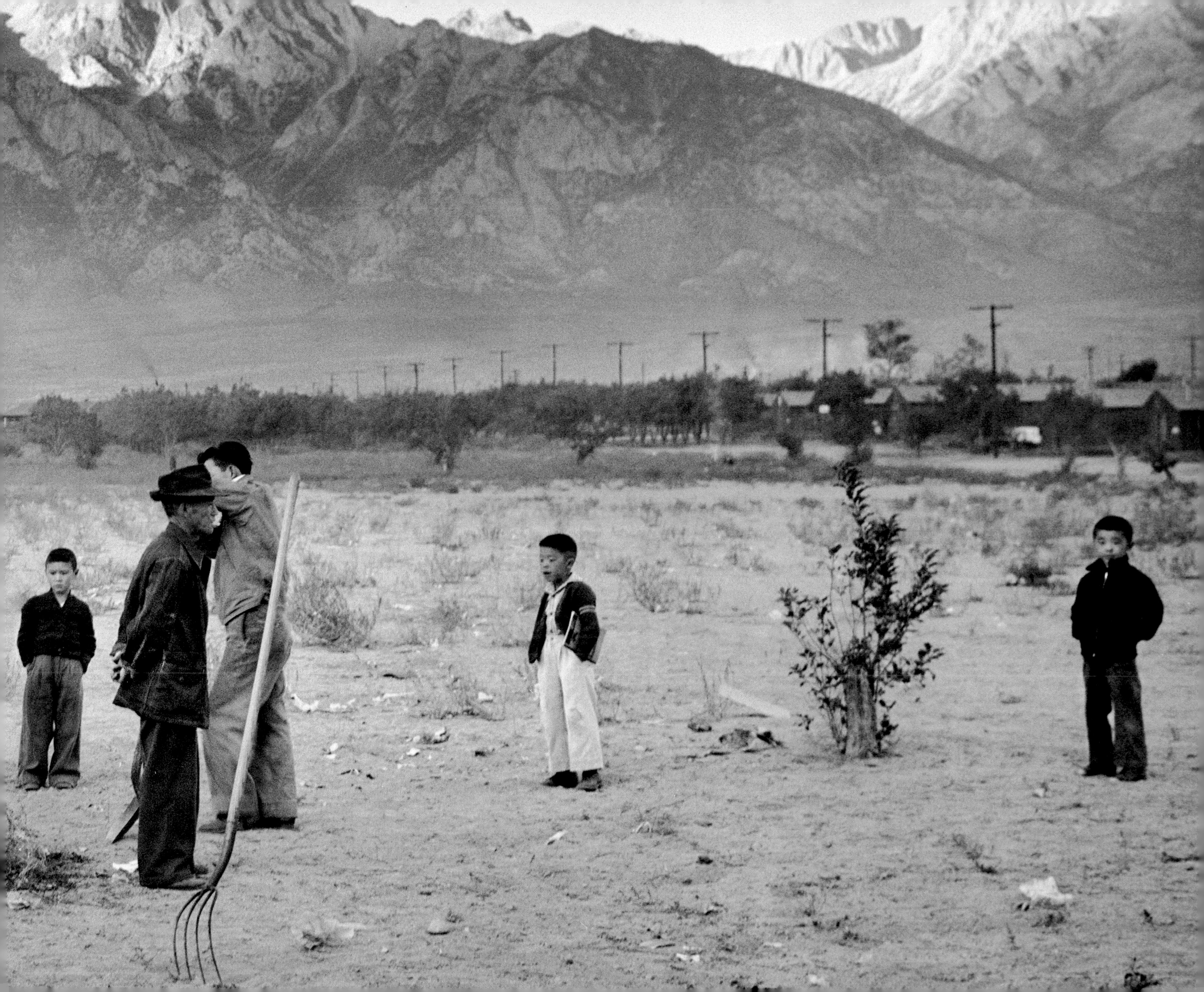

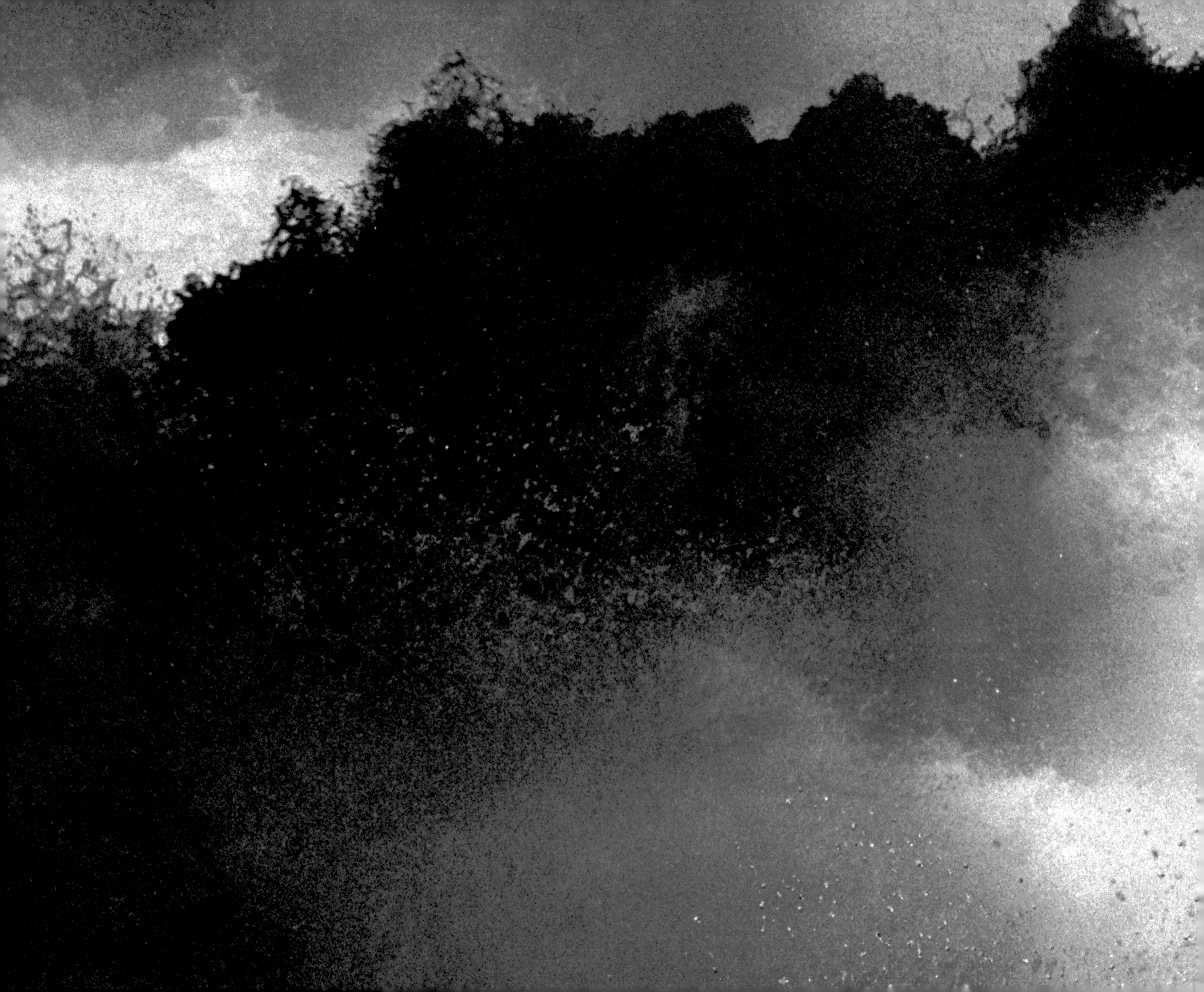

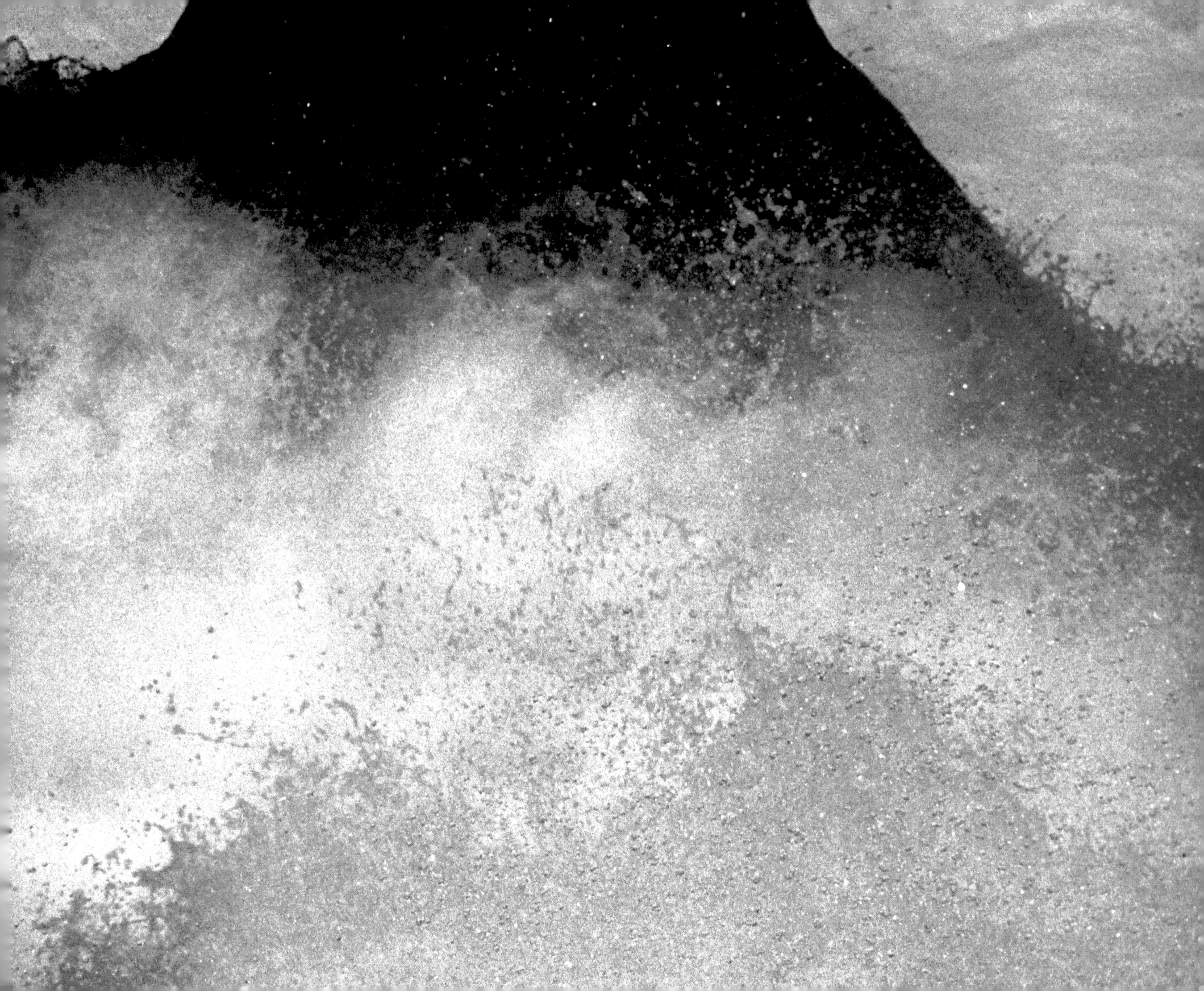

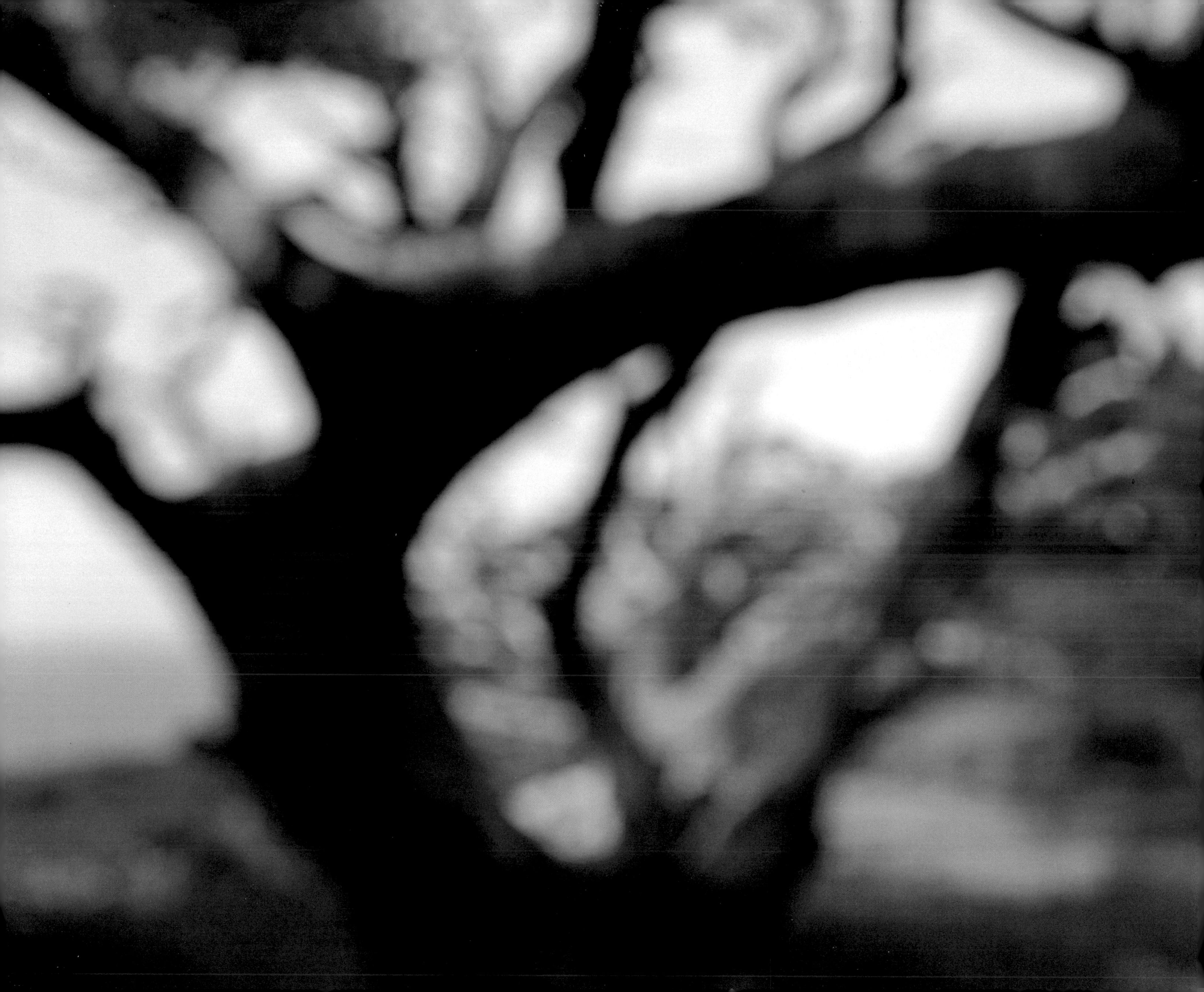

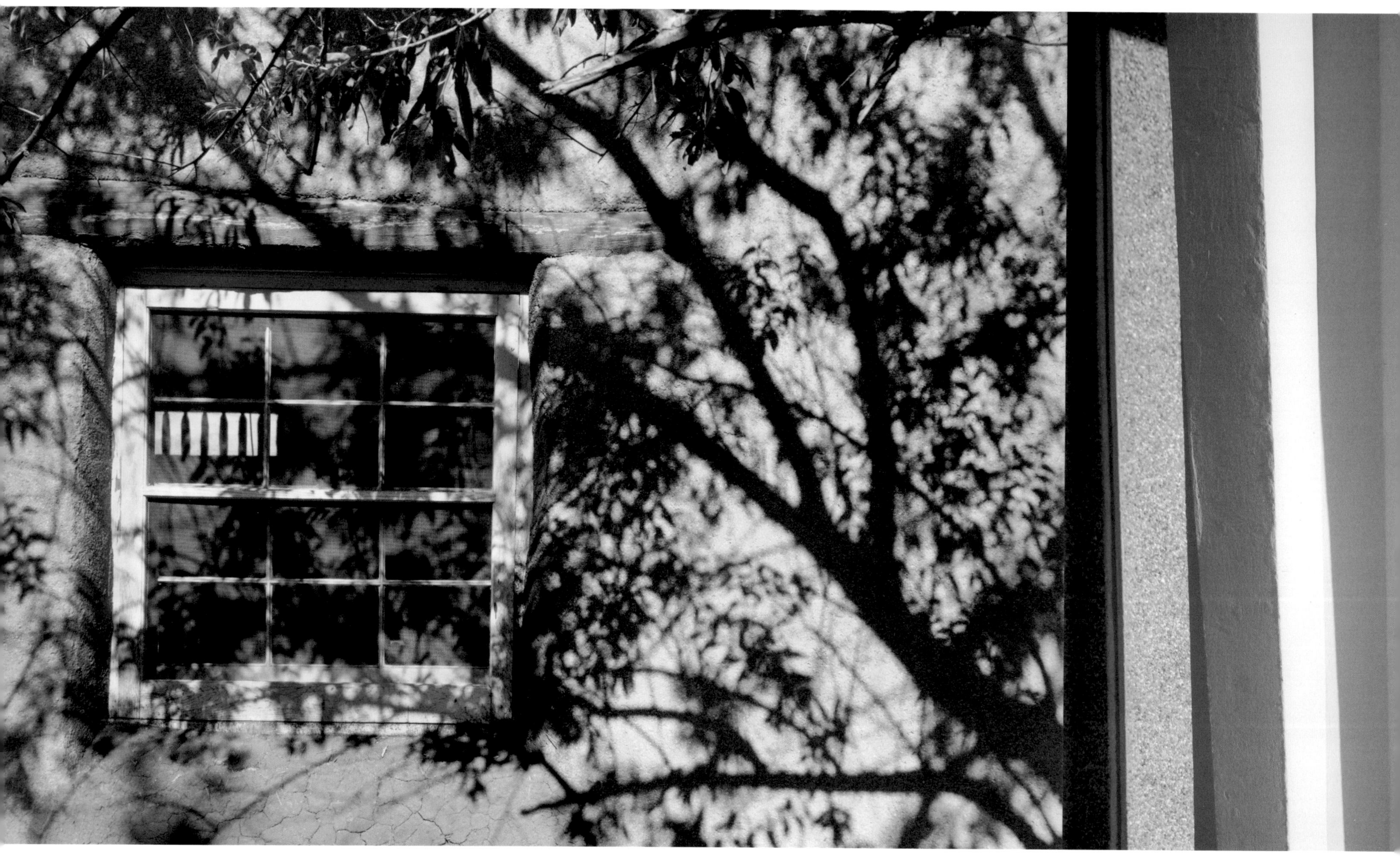

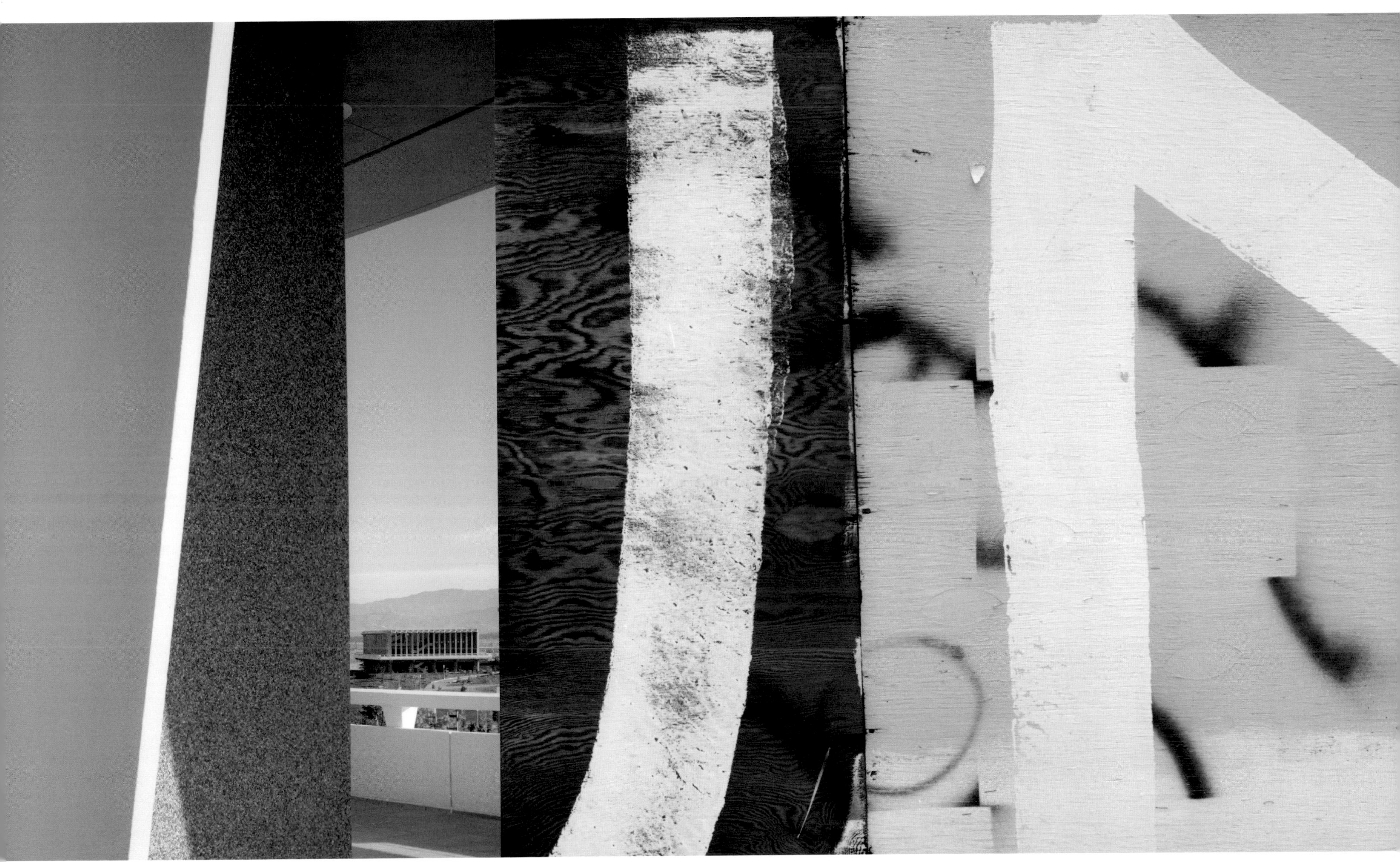

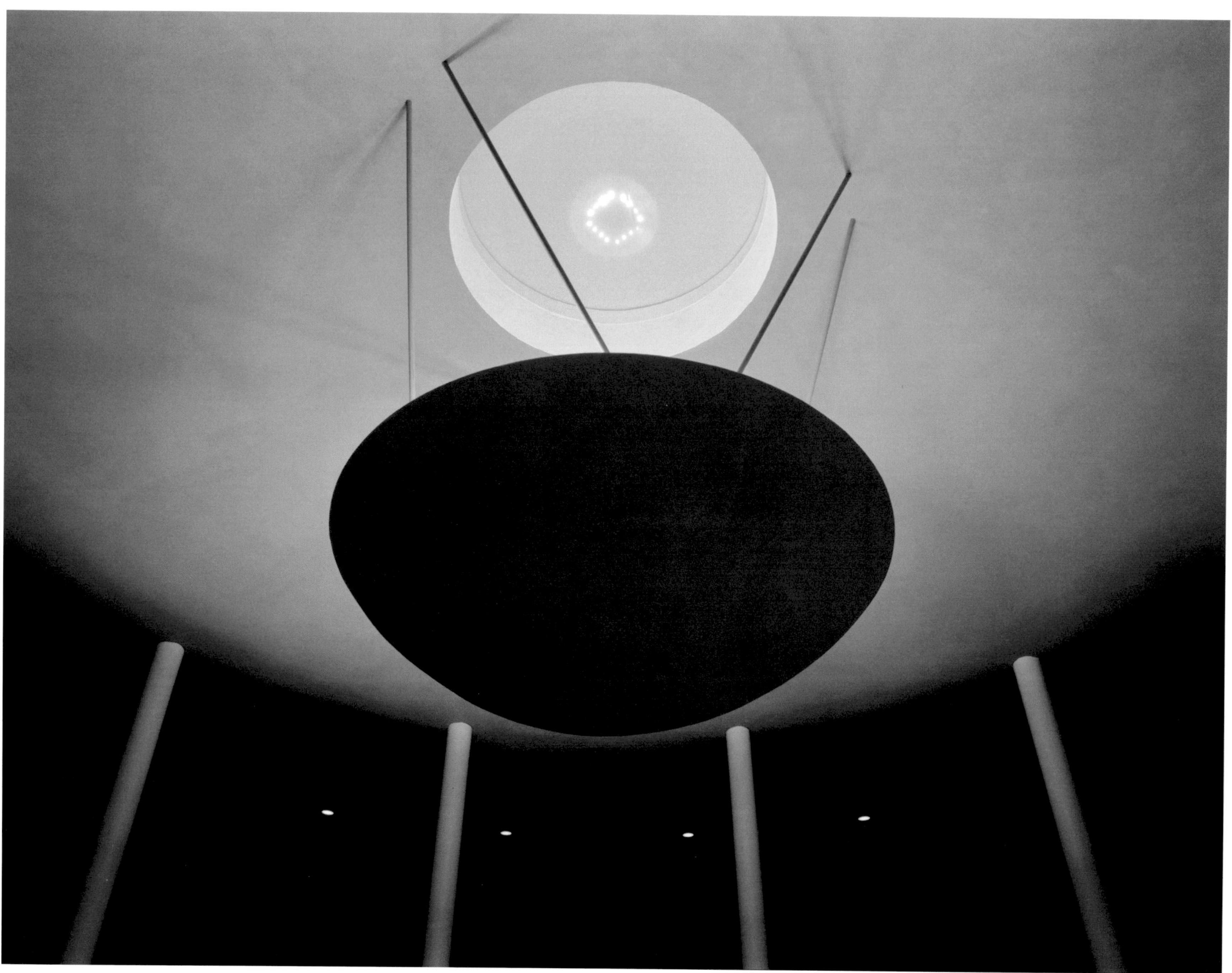

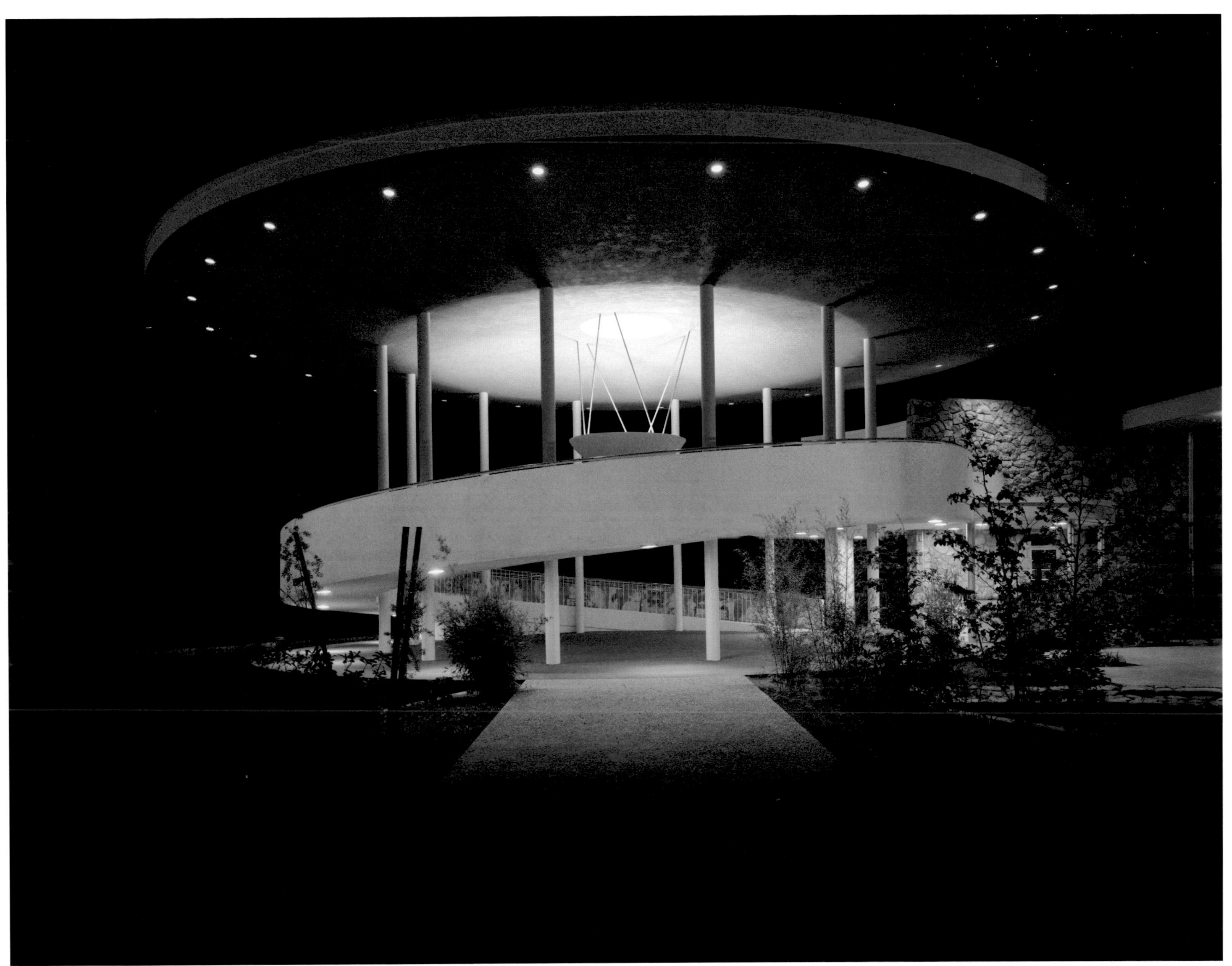

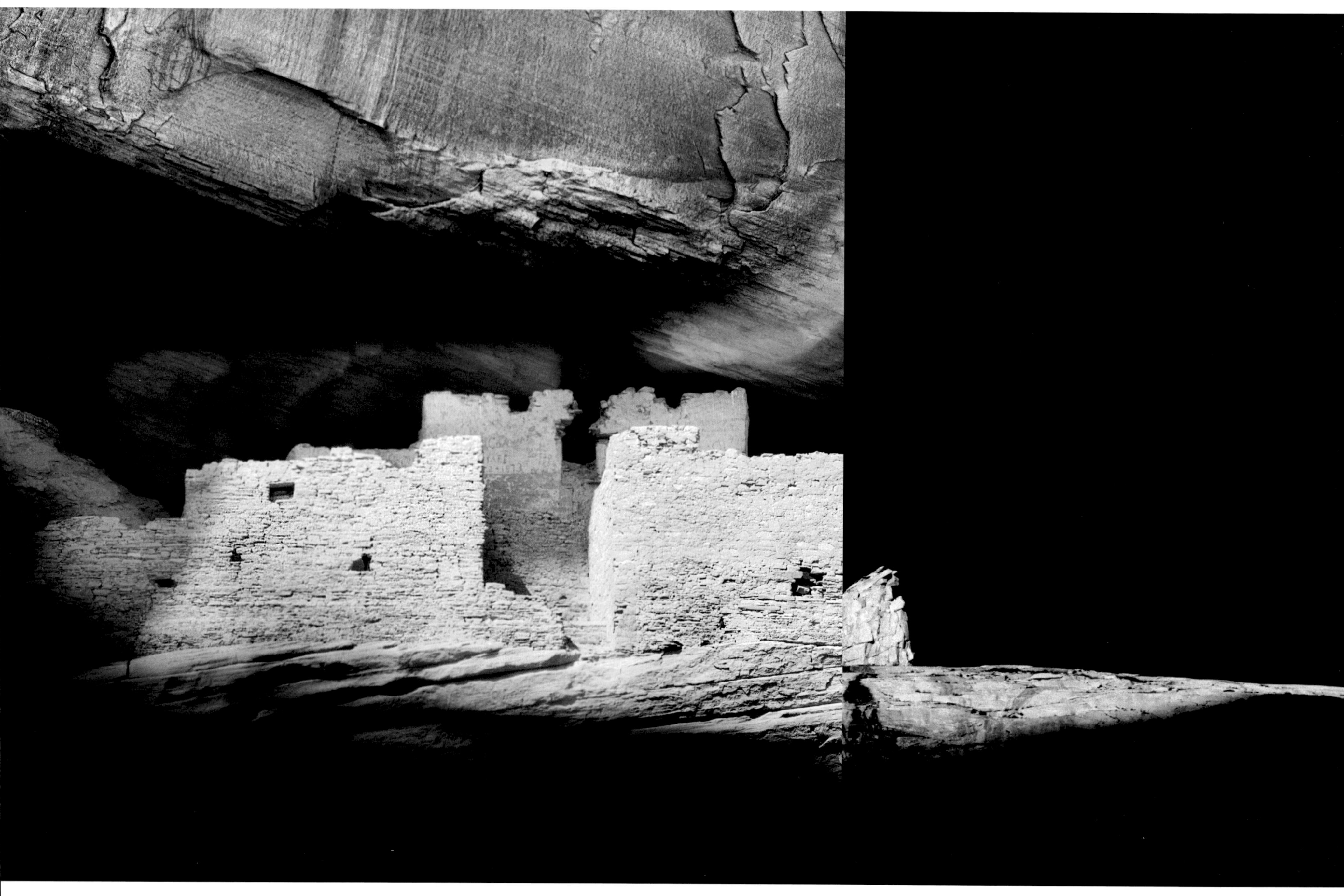

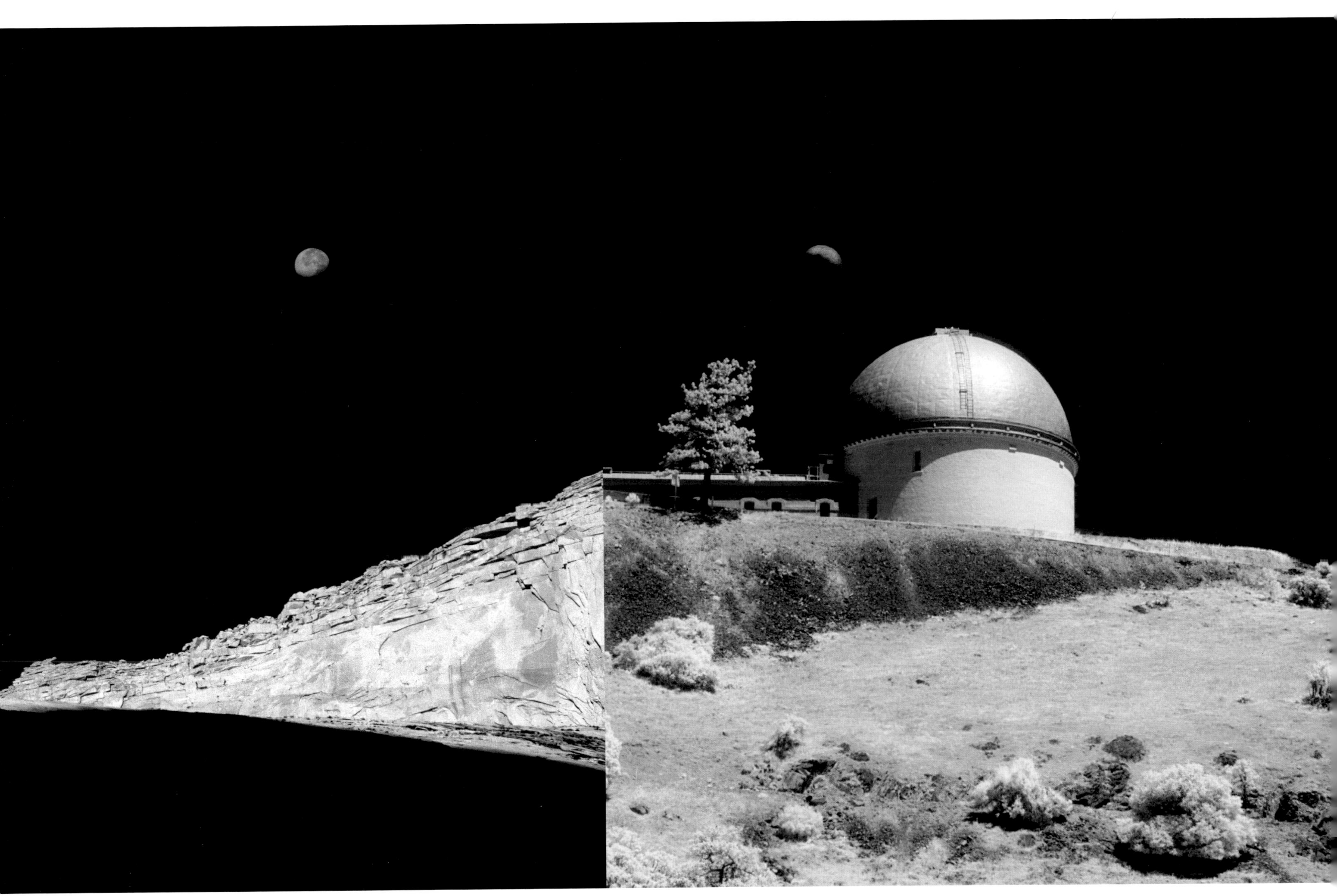

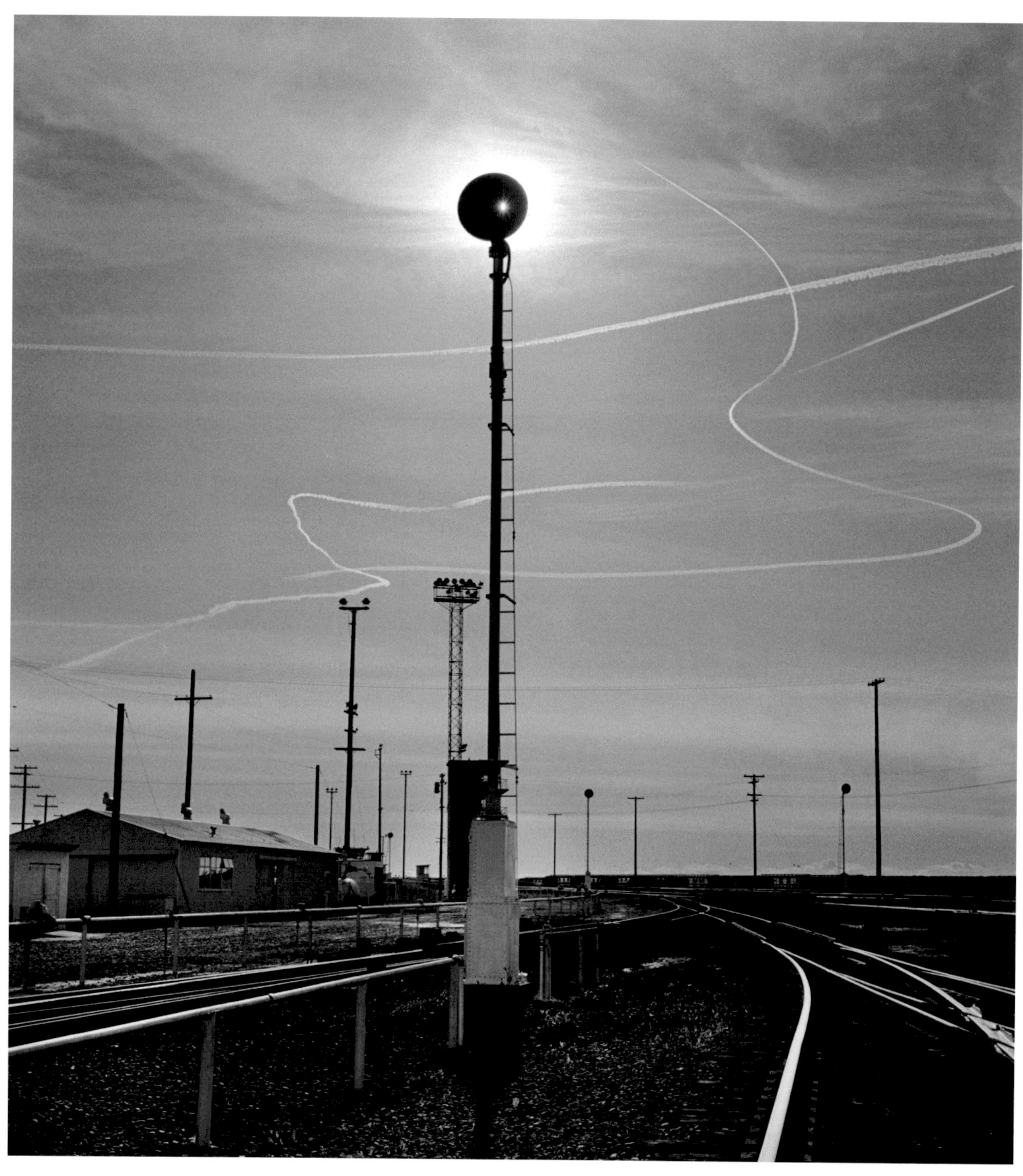

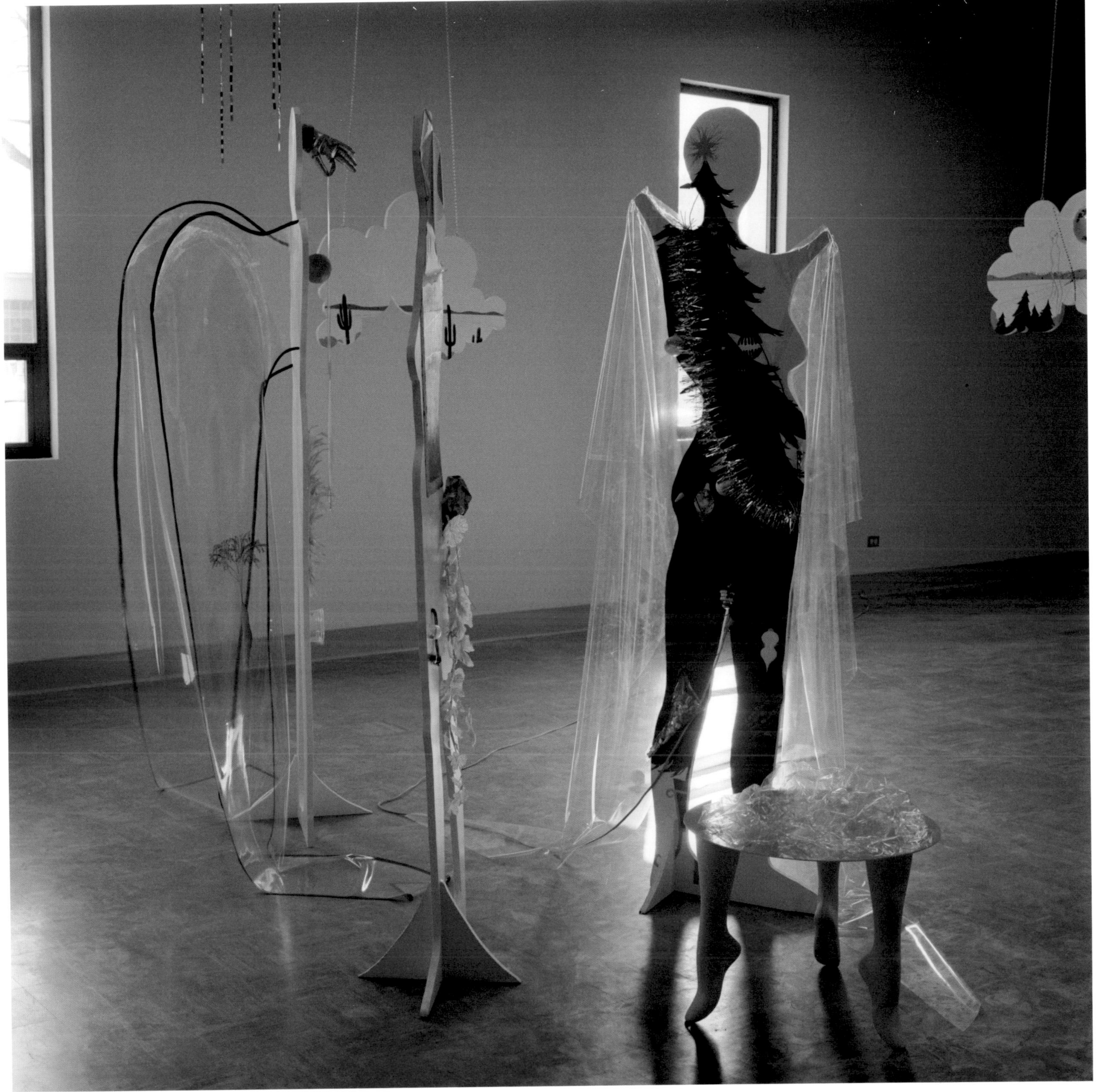

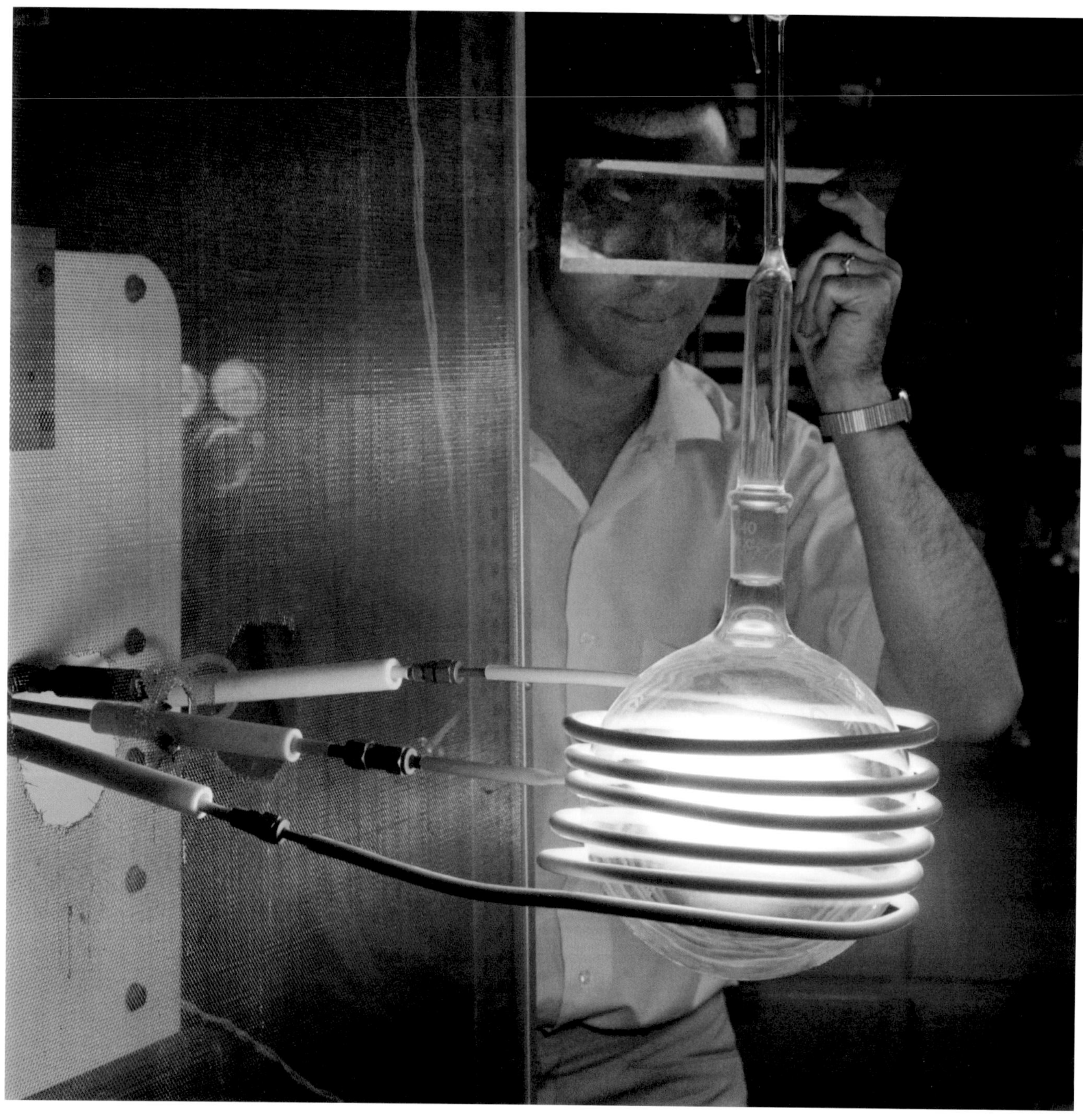

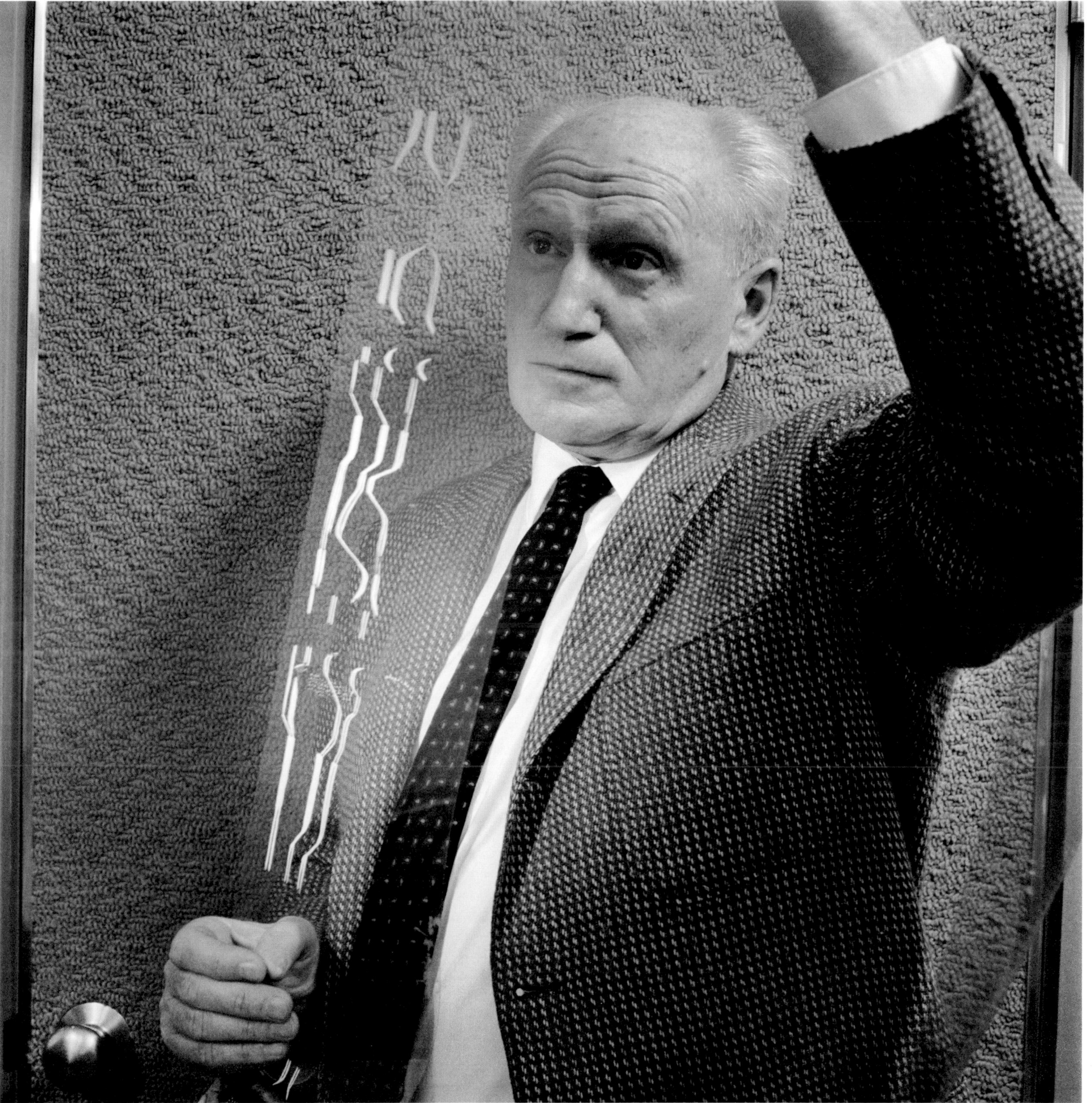

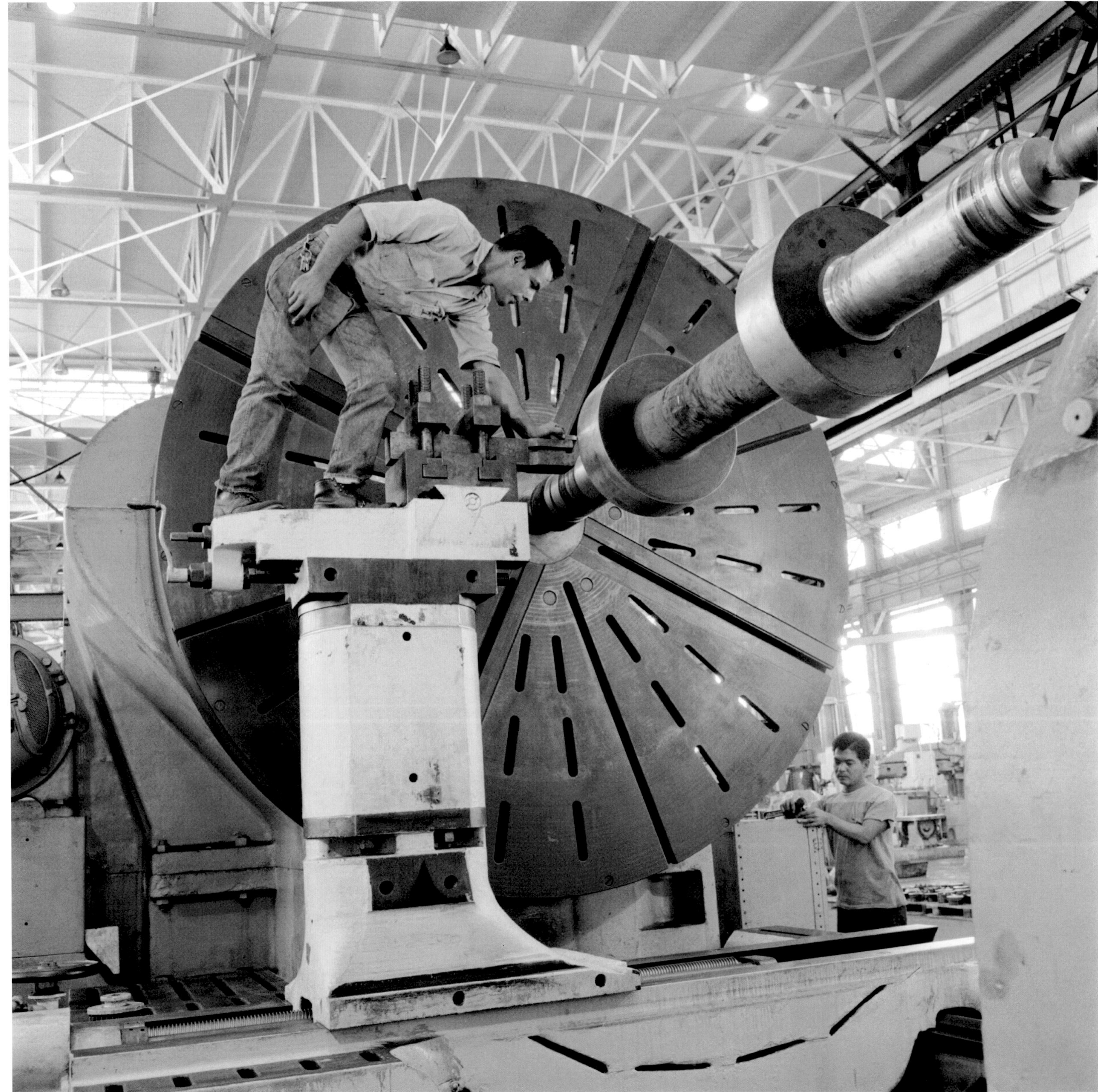

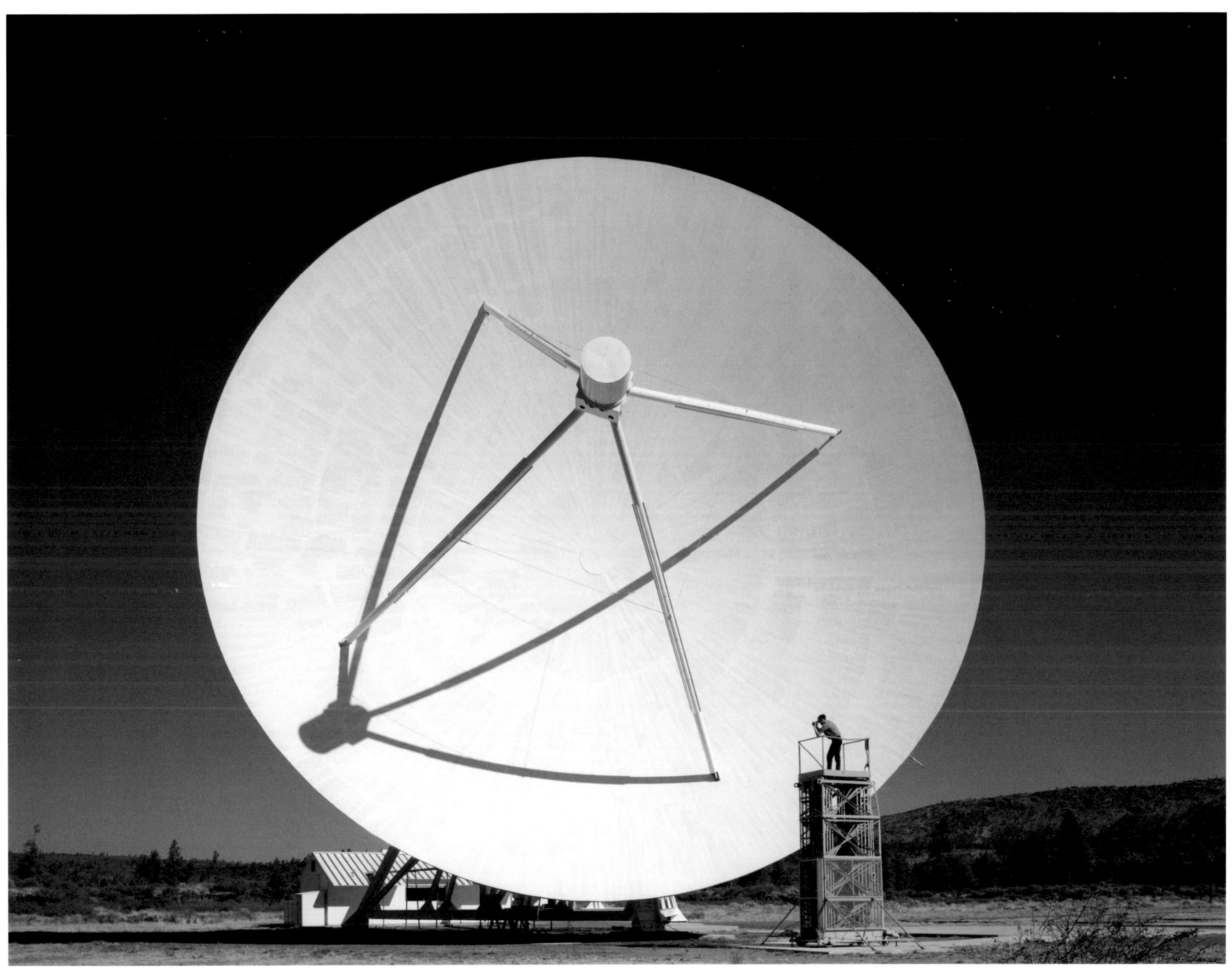

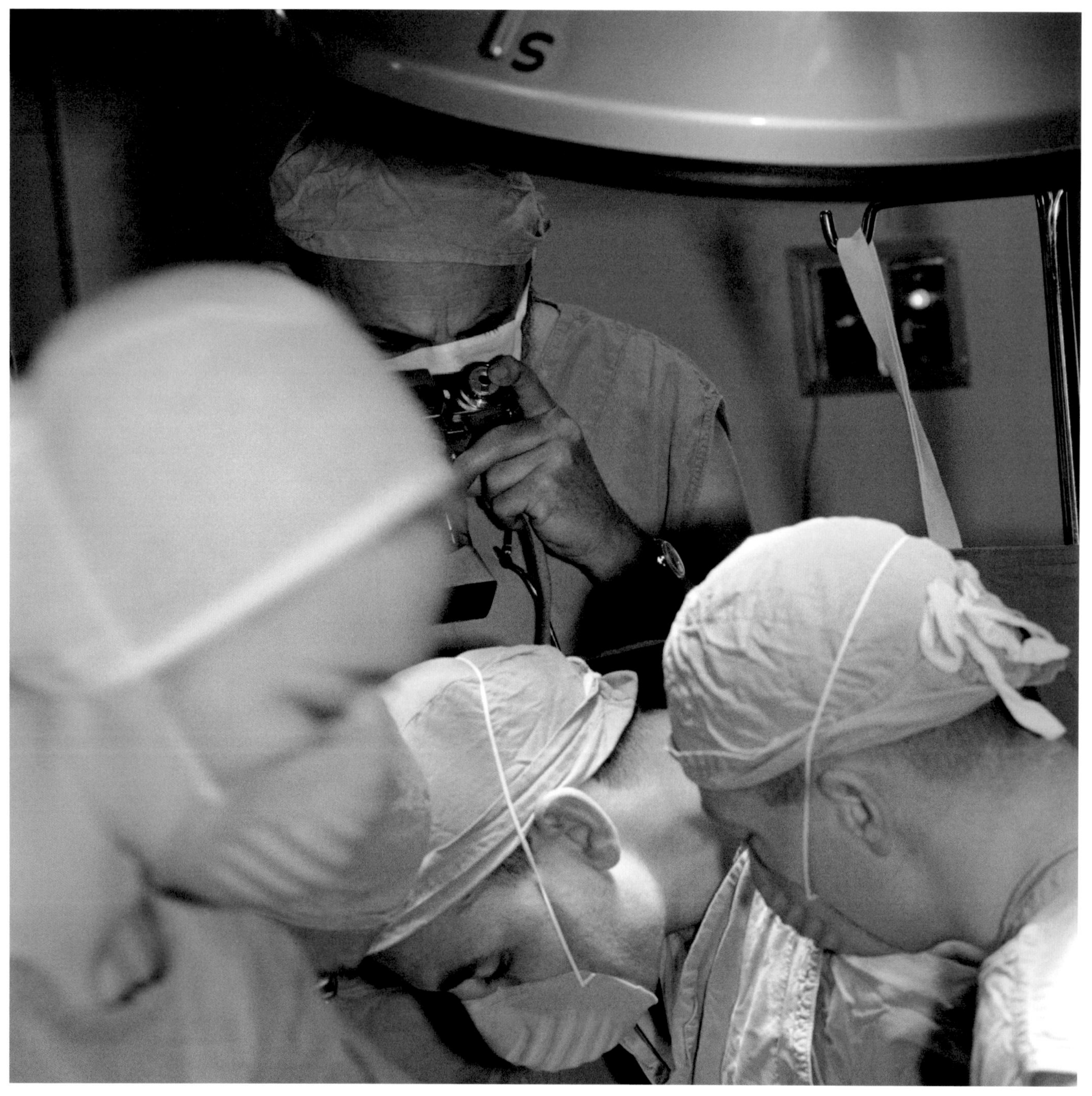

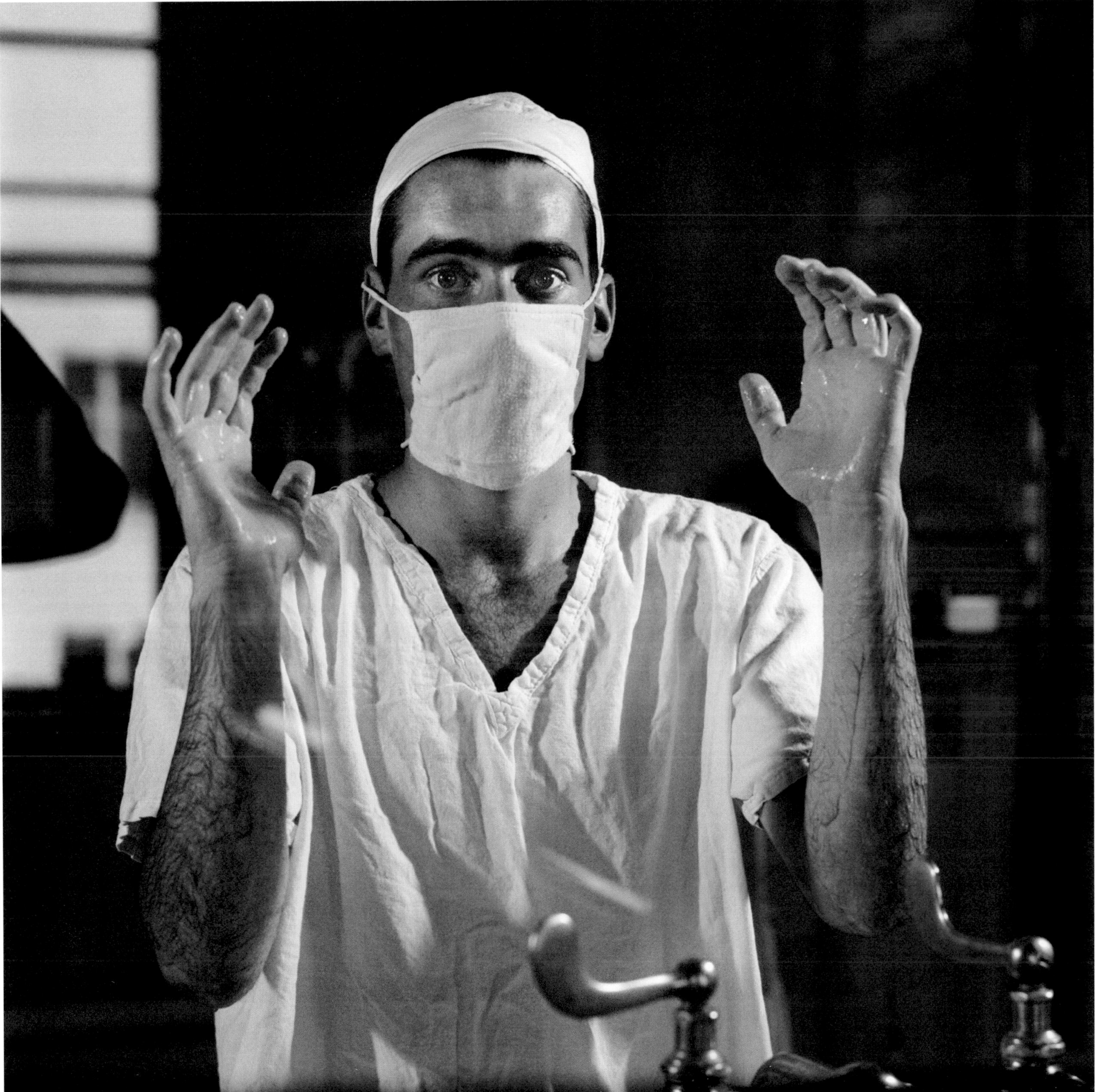

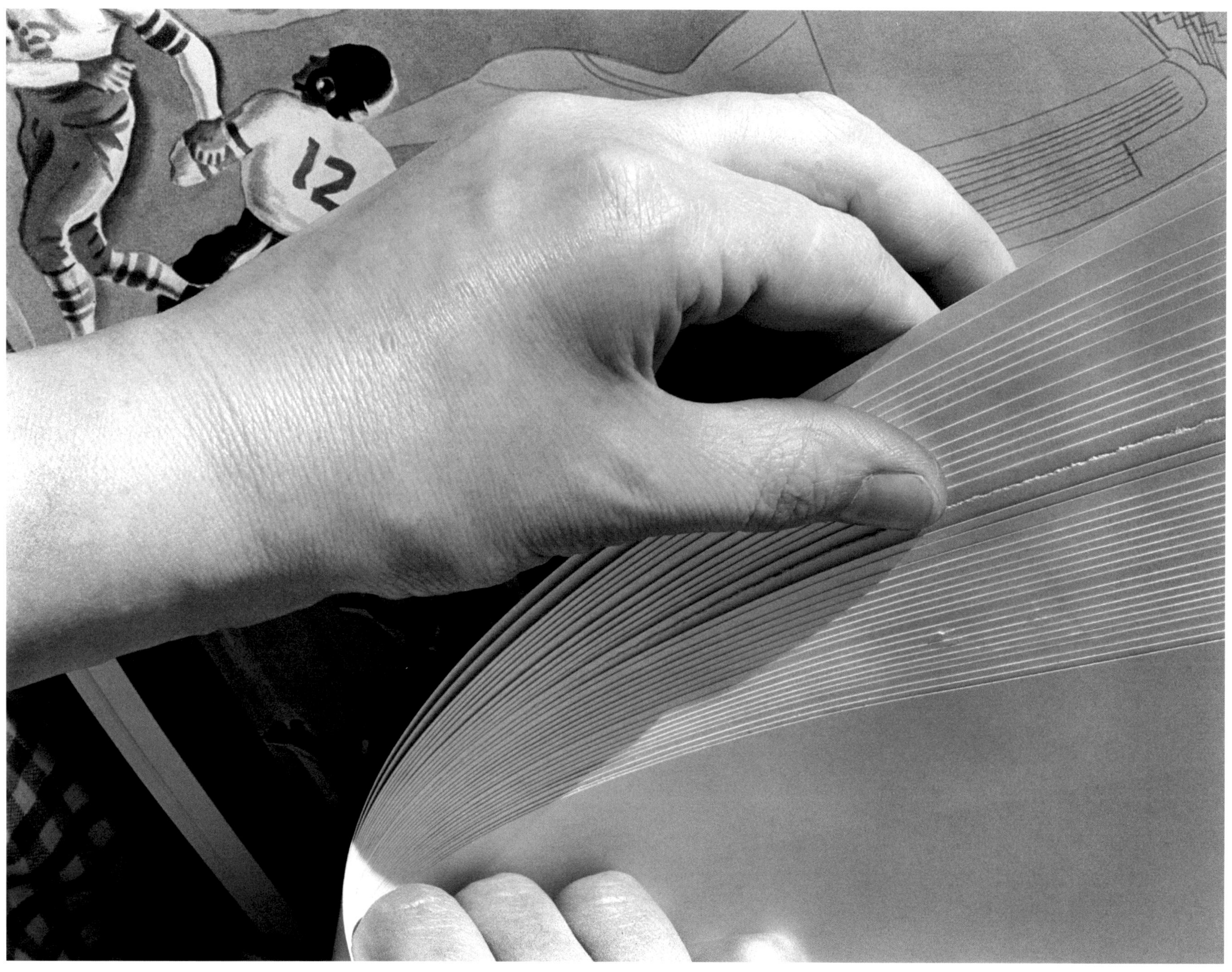

12

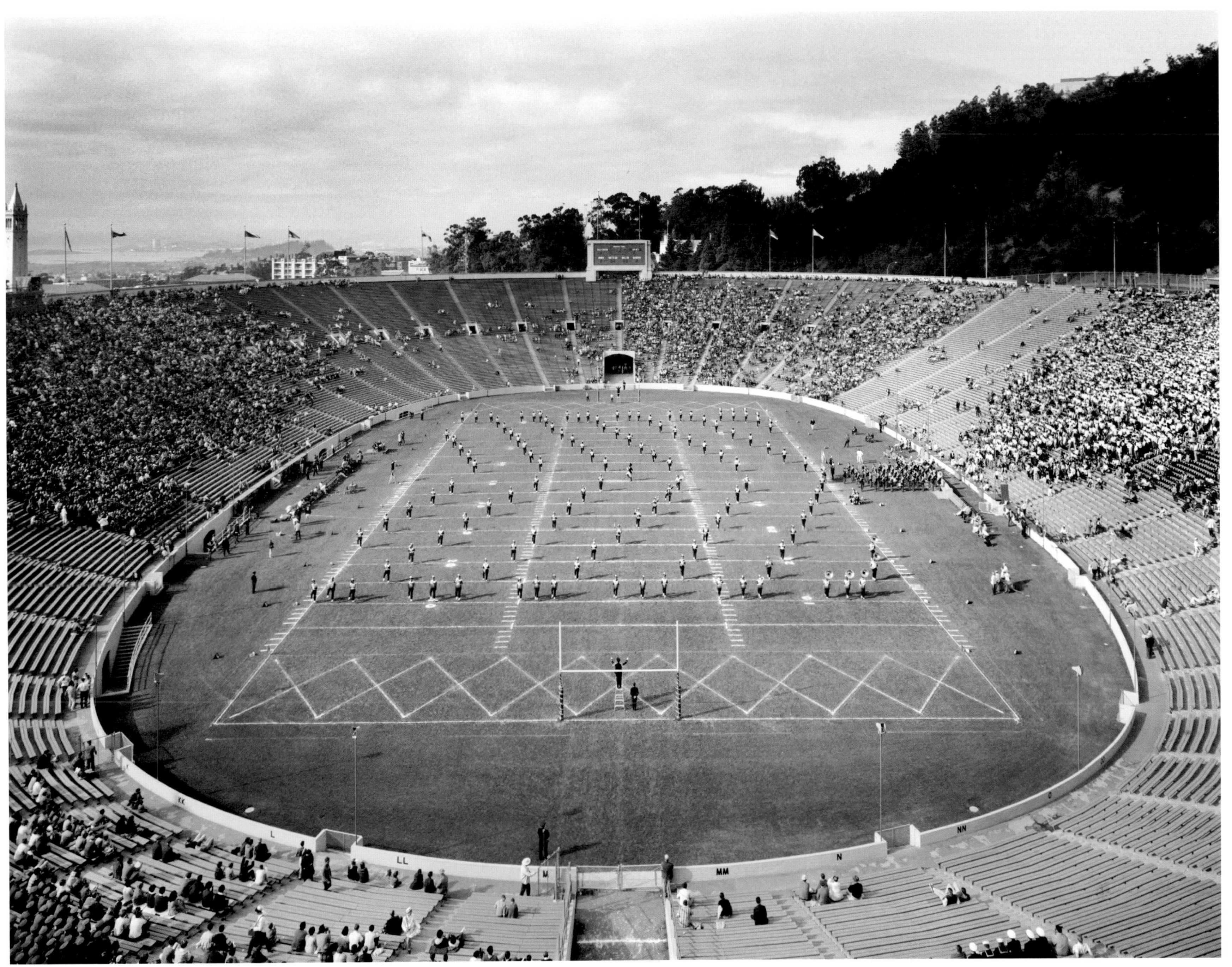

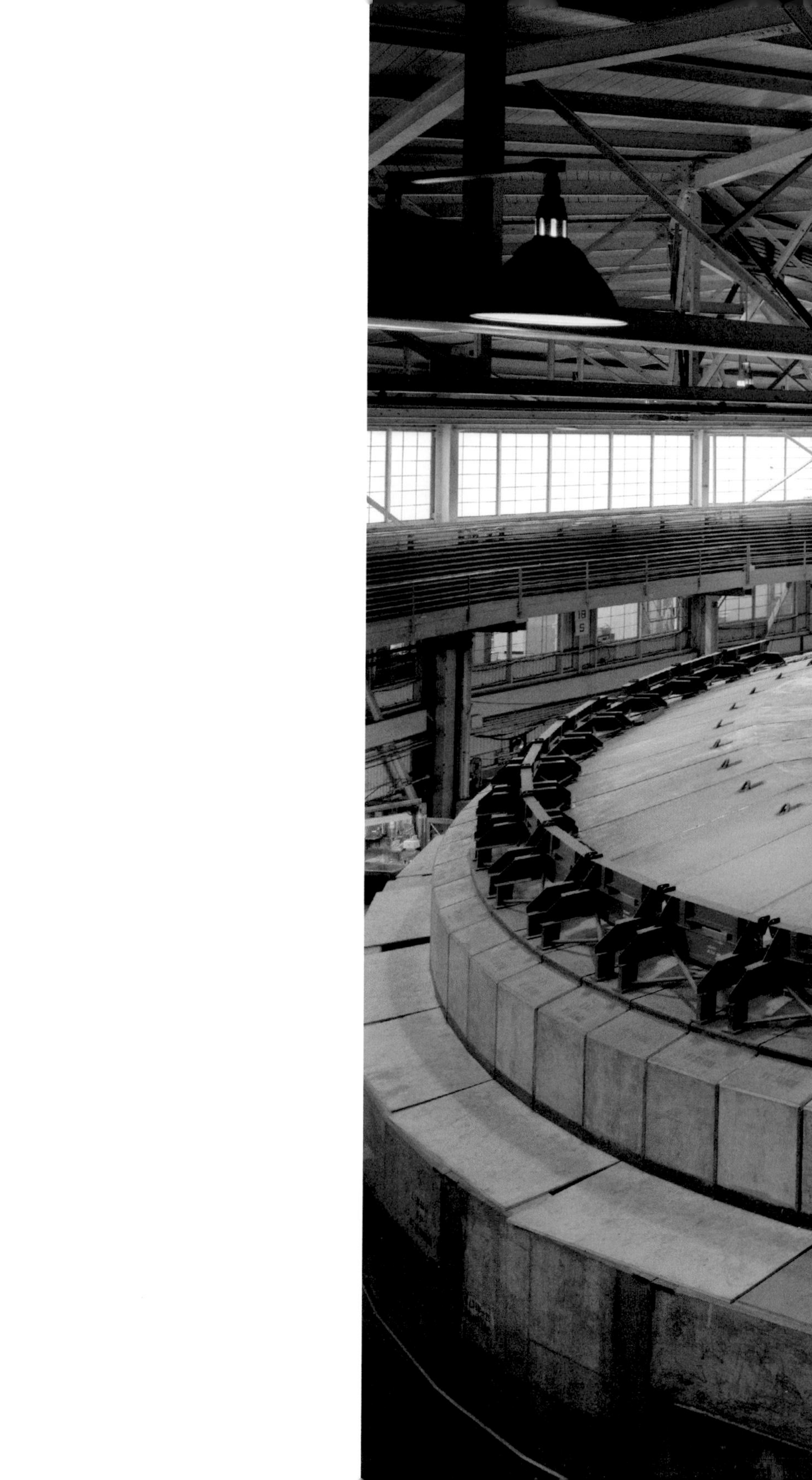

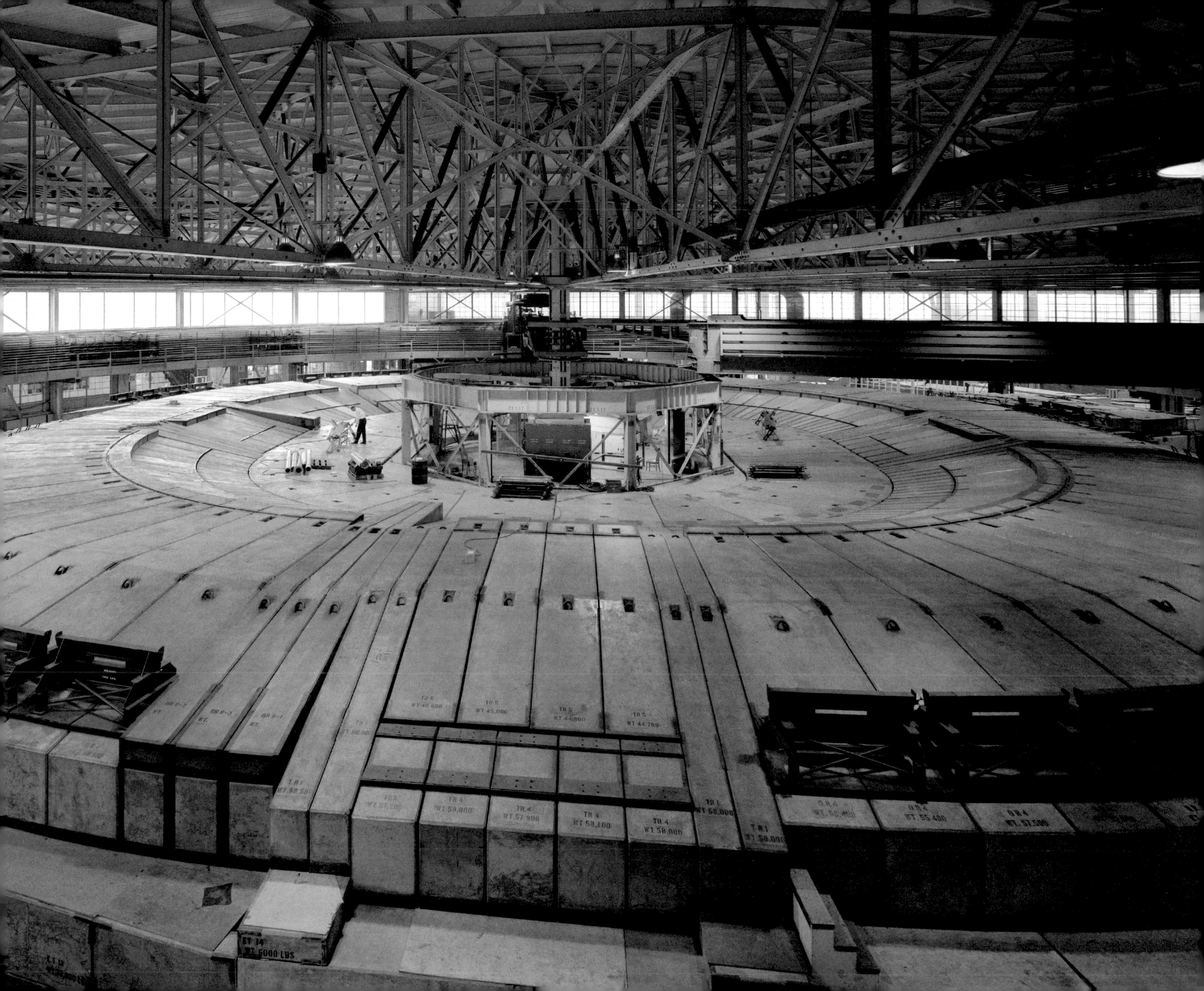

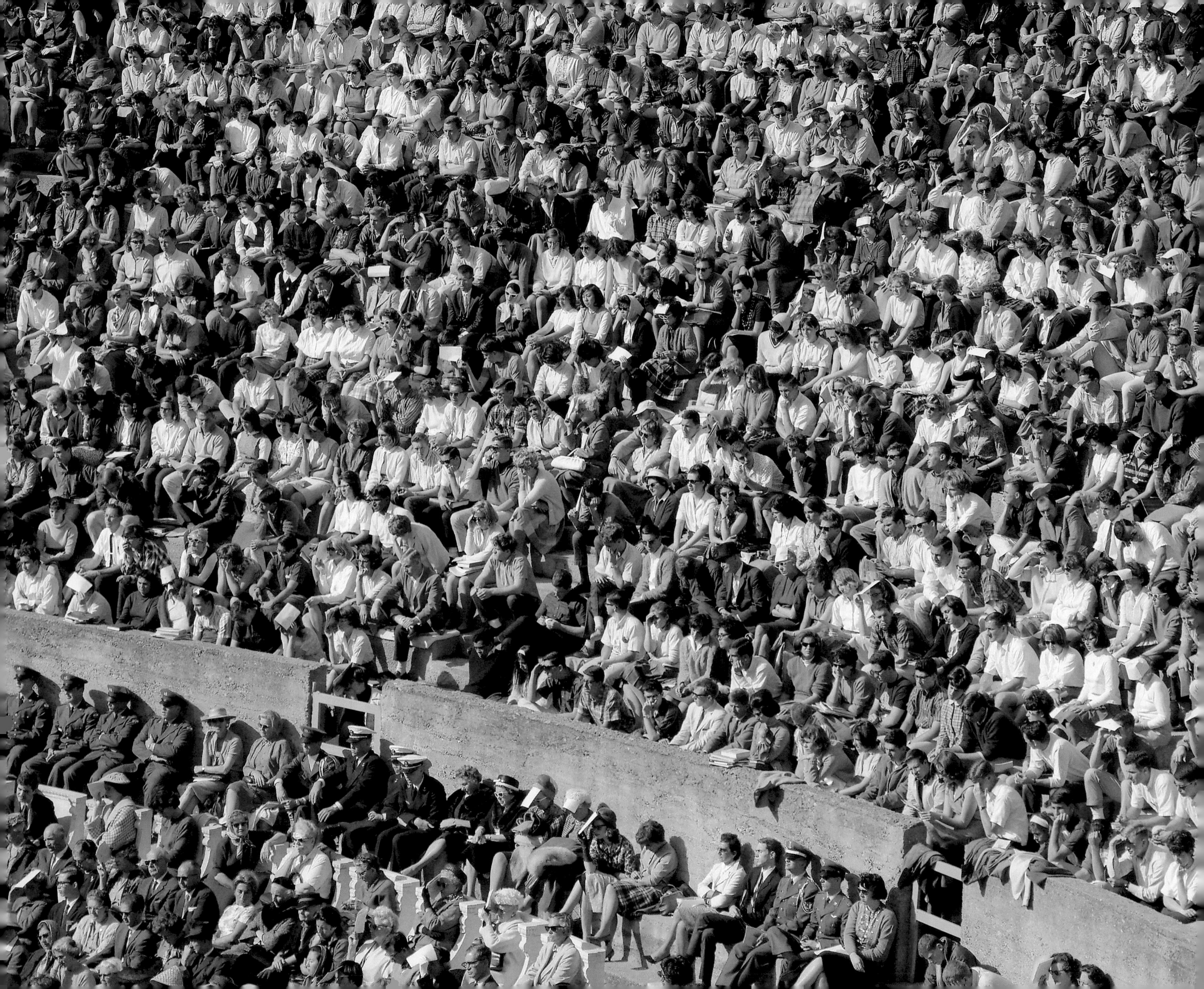

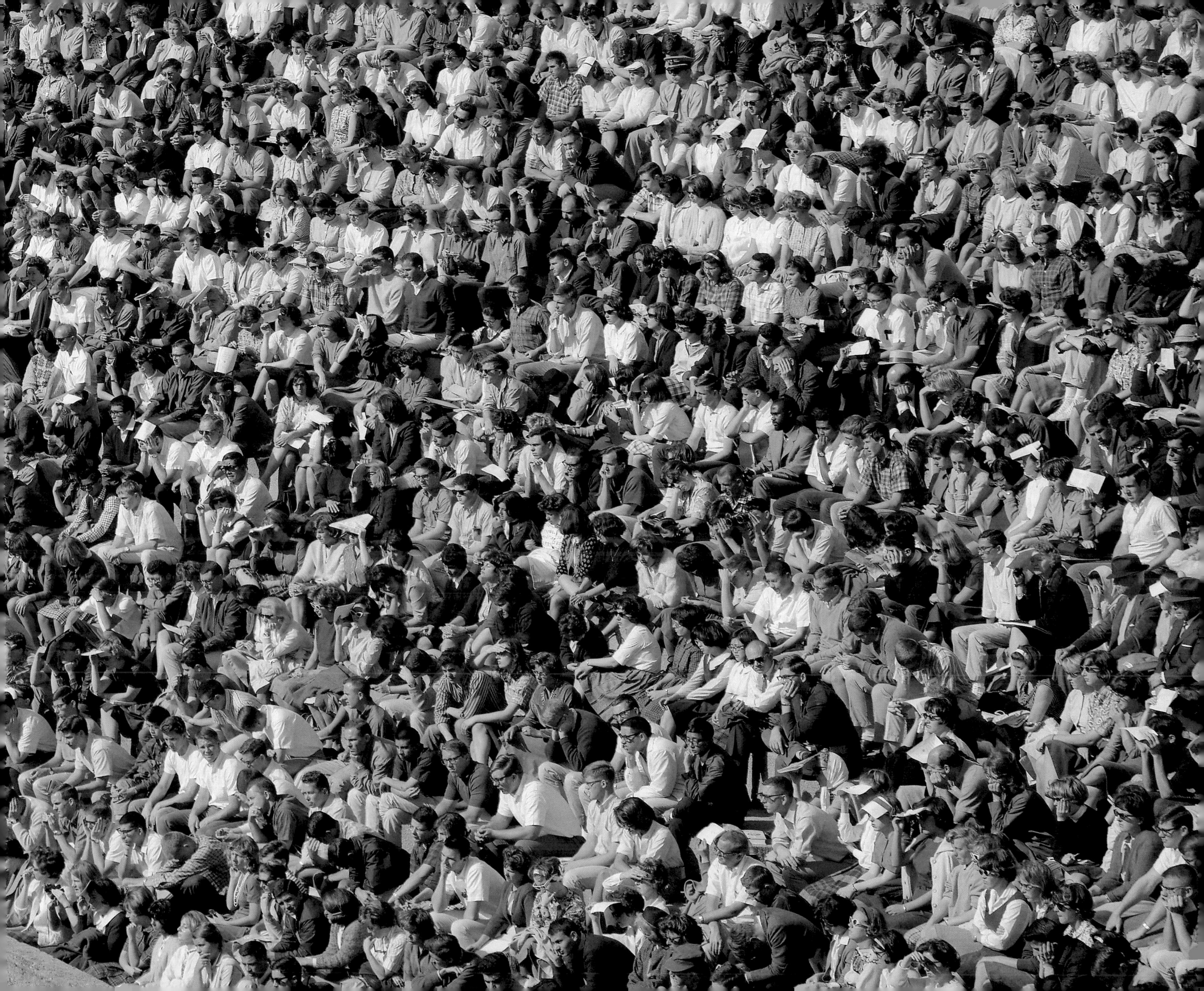

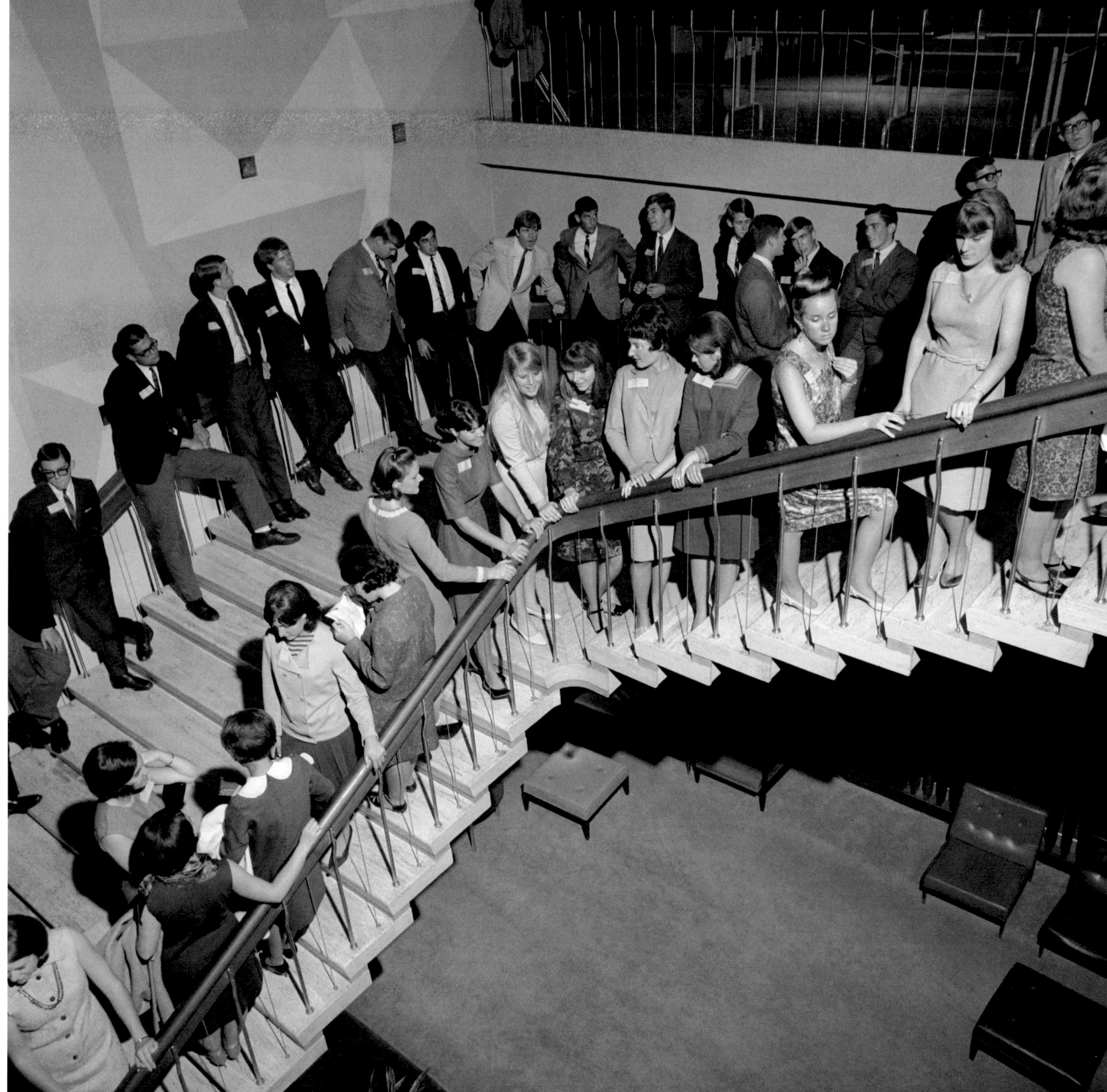

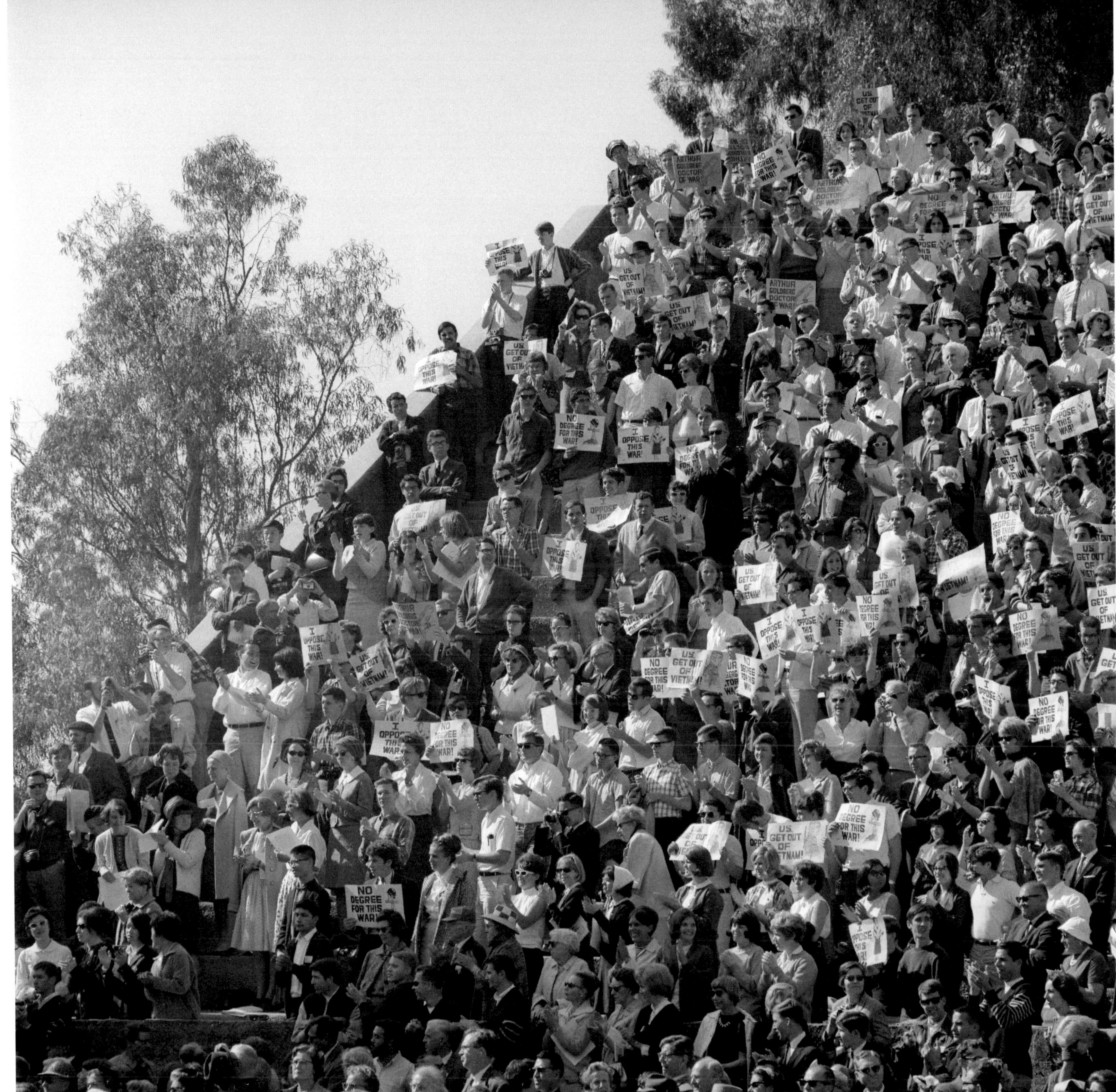
US GET OUT OF VIETNAM!
NO DEGREE FOR THIS WAR!
ARTHUR GOLDBERG DOCTOR OF WAR!
I OPPOSE THIS WAR!

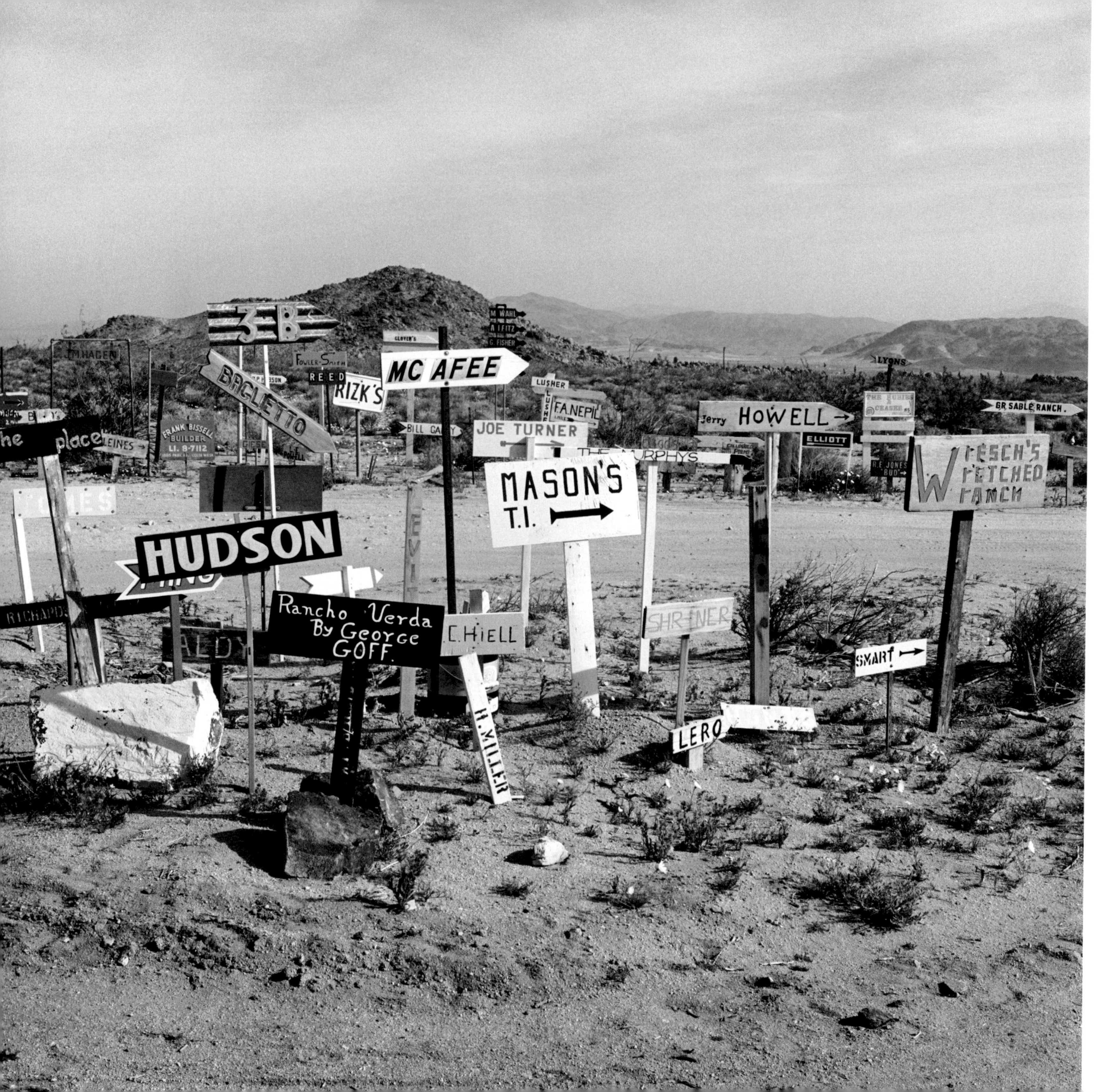

3-B
MC AFEE
BAGLIETTO
RIZK'S
REED
GLOVER'S
FOWLER-SMITH
M. HAGEN
FRANK BISSELL BUILDER
LI. 8-7112
the place
LEINES
BILL GARY
JOE TURNER
LUSHER
F.A. NEPIL
M. WAHL
A. FITZ
G. FISHER
THE MURPHYS
Jerry HOWELL
ELLIOTT
LYONS
THE RUBIS
CEASER #3
GR SABLE RANCH
R.E. JONES RUD
Wresch's Wretched Ranch
HUDSON
RICHARDS
Rancho Verda By George GOFF.
C. HIELL
MASON'S T.I.
SHRINER
SMART
H. MILLER
LERO

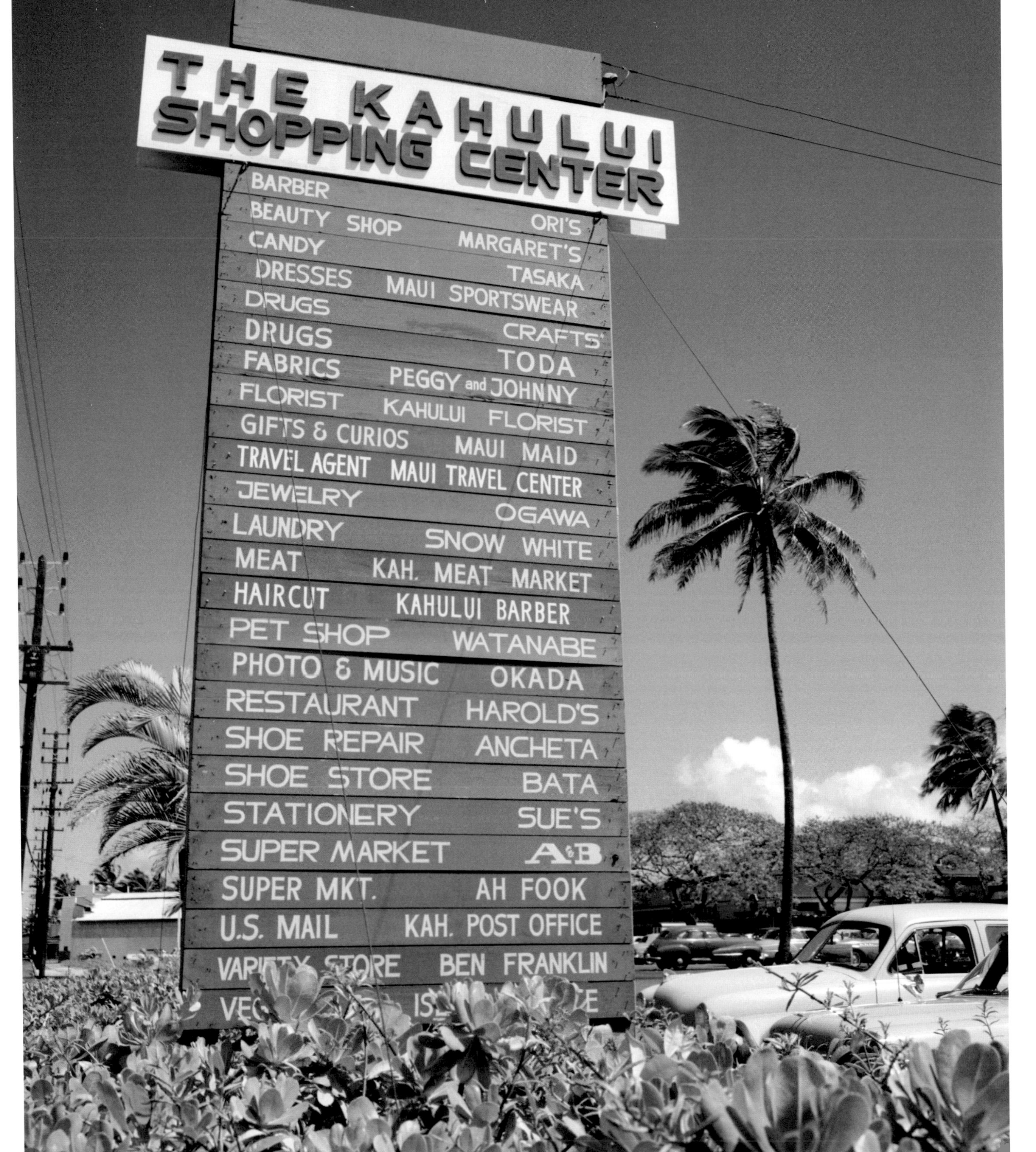

THE KAHULUI
SHOPPING CENTER
BARBER
BEAUTY SHOP   ORI'S
CANDY   MARGARET'S
DRESSES   TASAKA
DRUGS   MAUI SPORTSWEAR
DRUGS   CRAFTS'
FABRICS   TODA
FLORIST   PEGGY and JOHNNY
FLORIST   KAHULUI FLORIST
GIFTS & CURIOS   MAUI MAID
TRAVEL AGENT MAUI TRAVEL CENTER
JEWELRY   OGAWA
LAUNDRY   SNOW WHITE
MEAT   KAH. MEAT MARKET
HAIRCUT   KAHULUI BARBER
PET SHOP   WATANABE
PHOTO & MUSIC   OKADA
RESTAURANT   HAROLD'S
SHOE REPAIR   ANCHETA
SHOE STORE   BATA
STATIONERY   SUE'S
SUPER MARKET   A&B
SUPER MKT.   AH FOOK
U.S. MAIL   KAH. POST OFFICE
VARIETY STORE   BEN FRANKLIN
VEG   ISL.

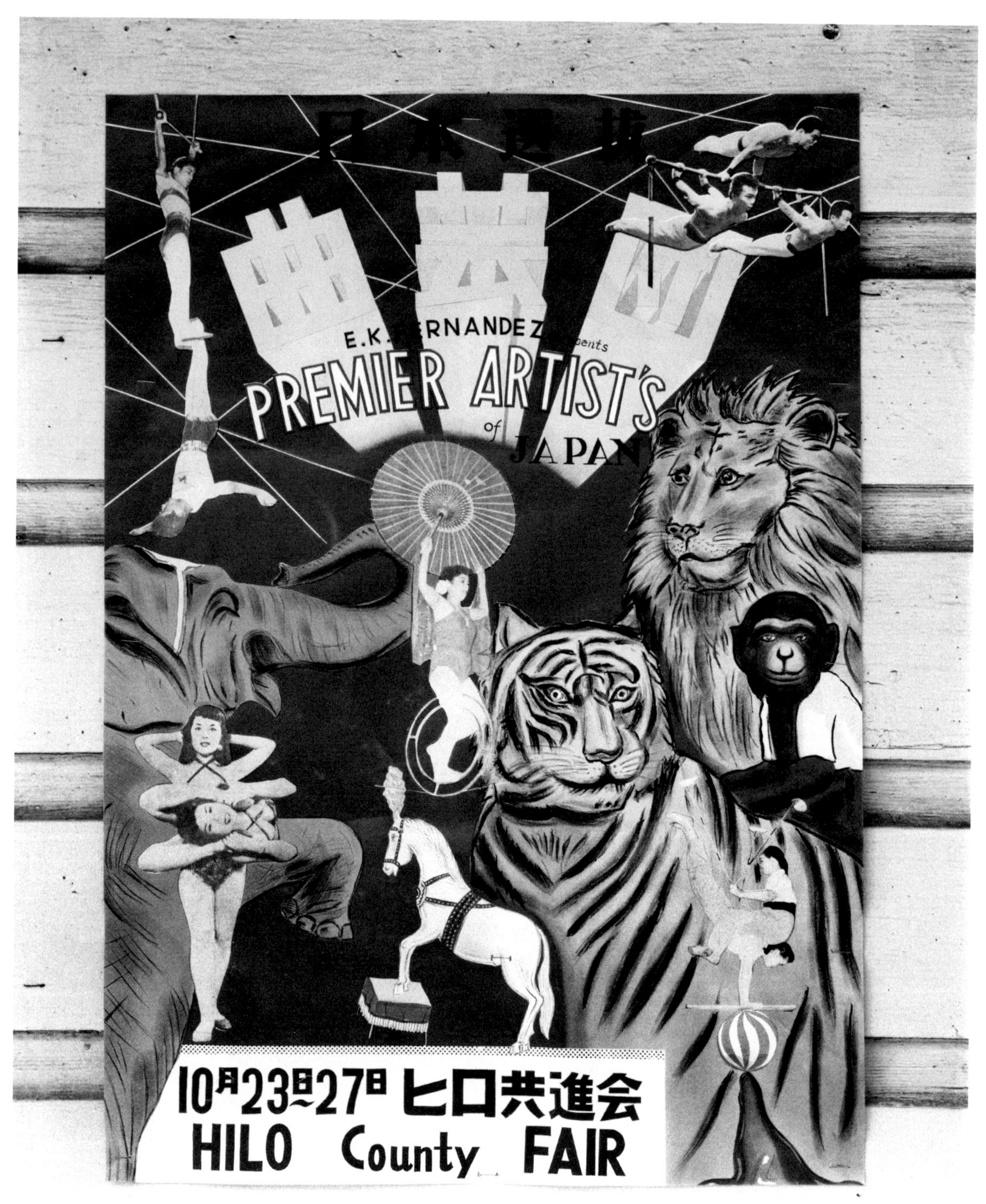
日本曲藝
曲藝團
E.K. FERNANDEZ presents
PREMIER ARTIST'S
of JAPAN
10月23日~27日 ヒロ共進会
HILO County FAIR

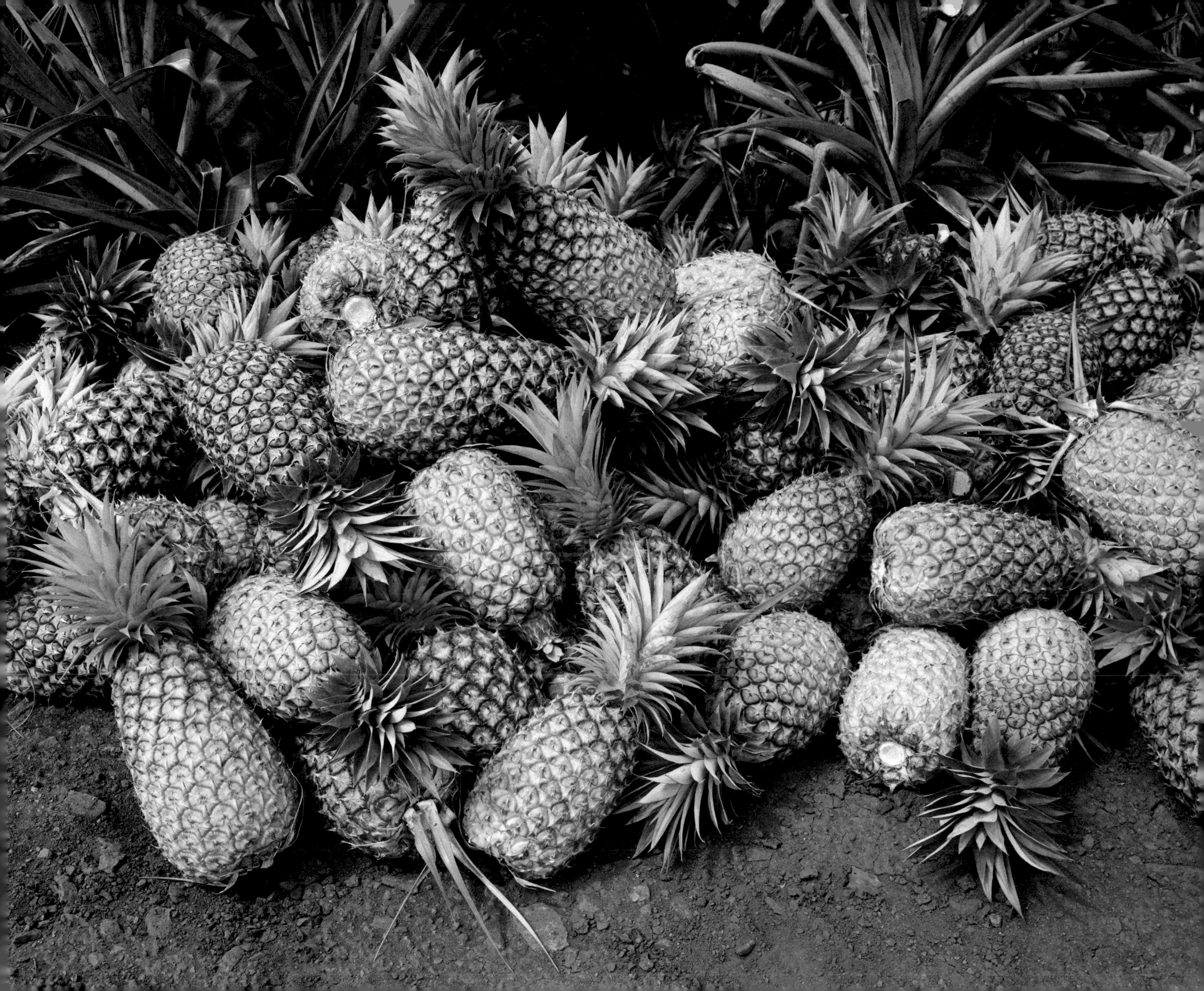

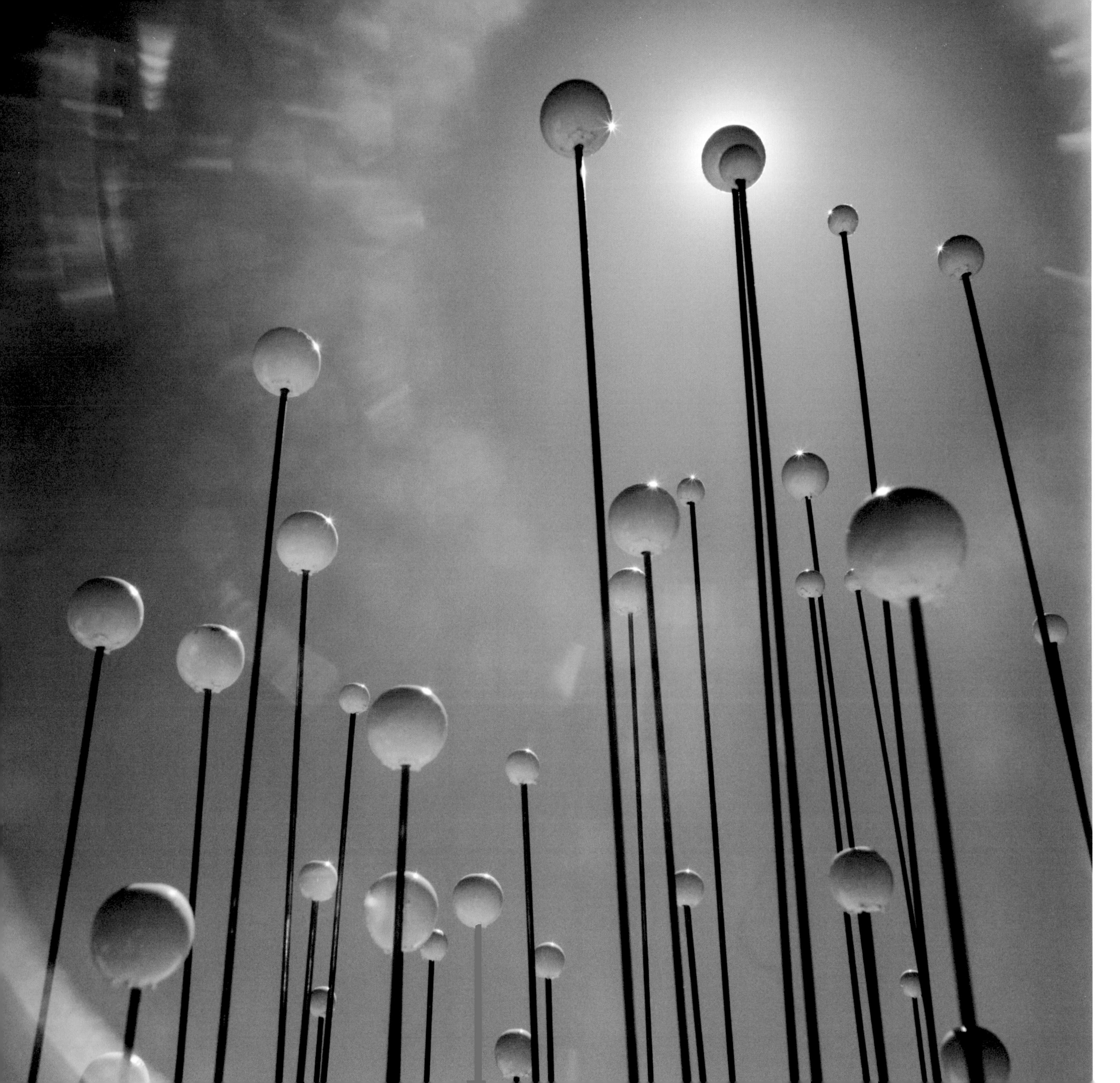

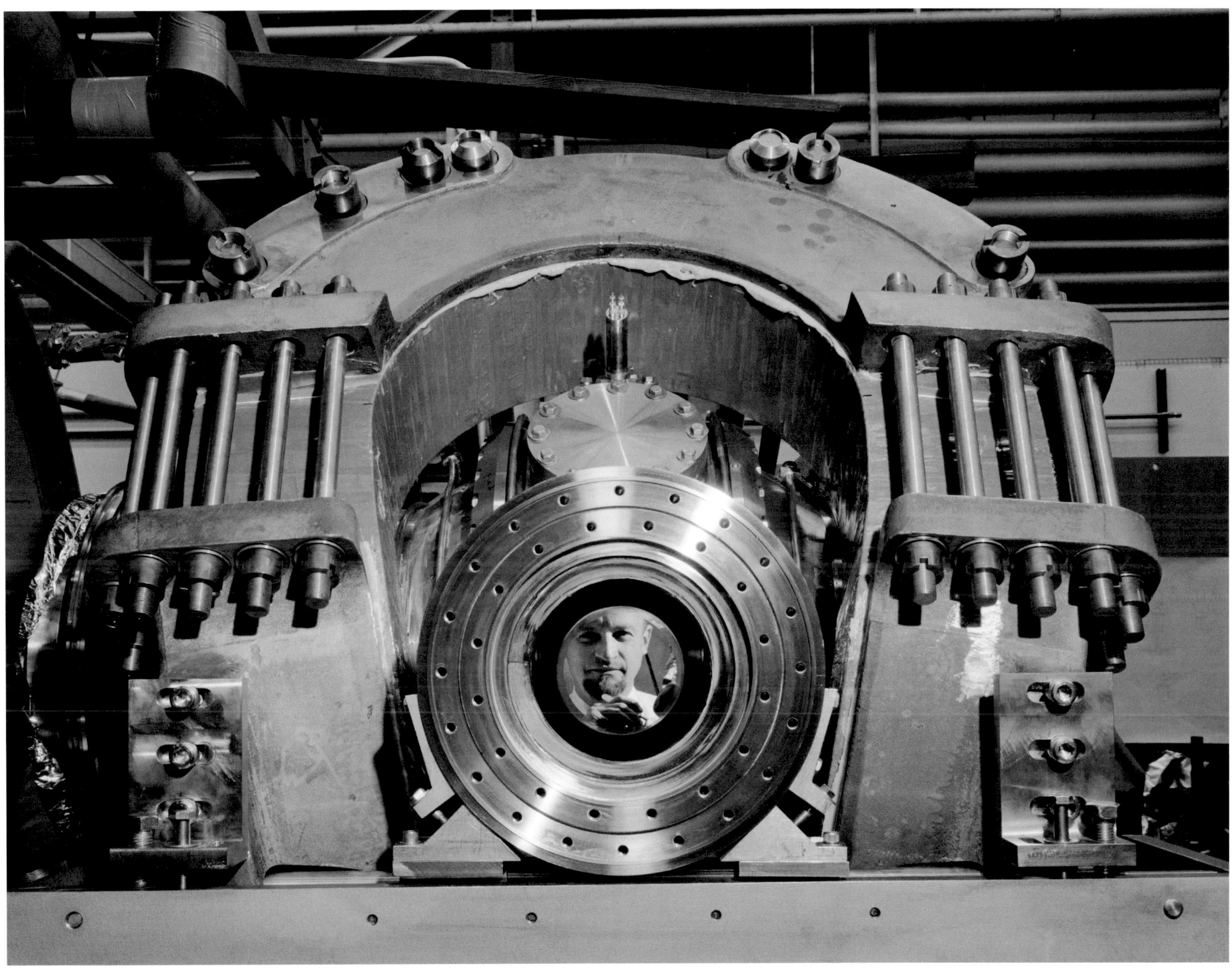

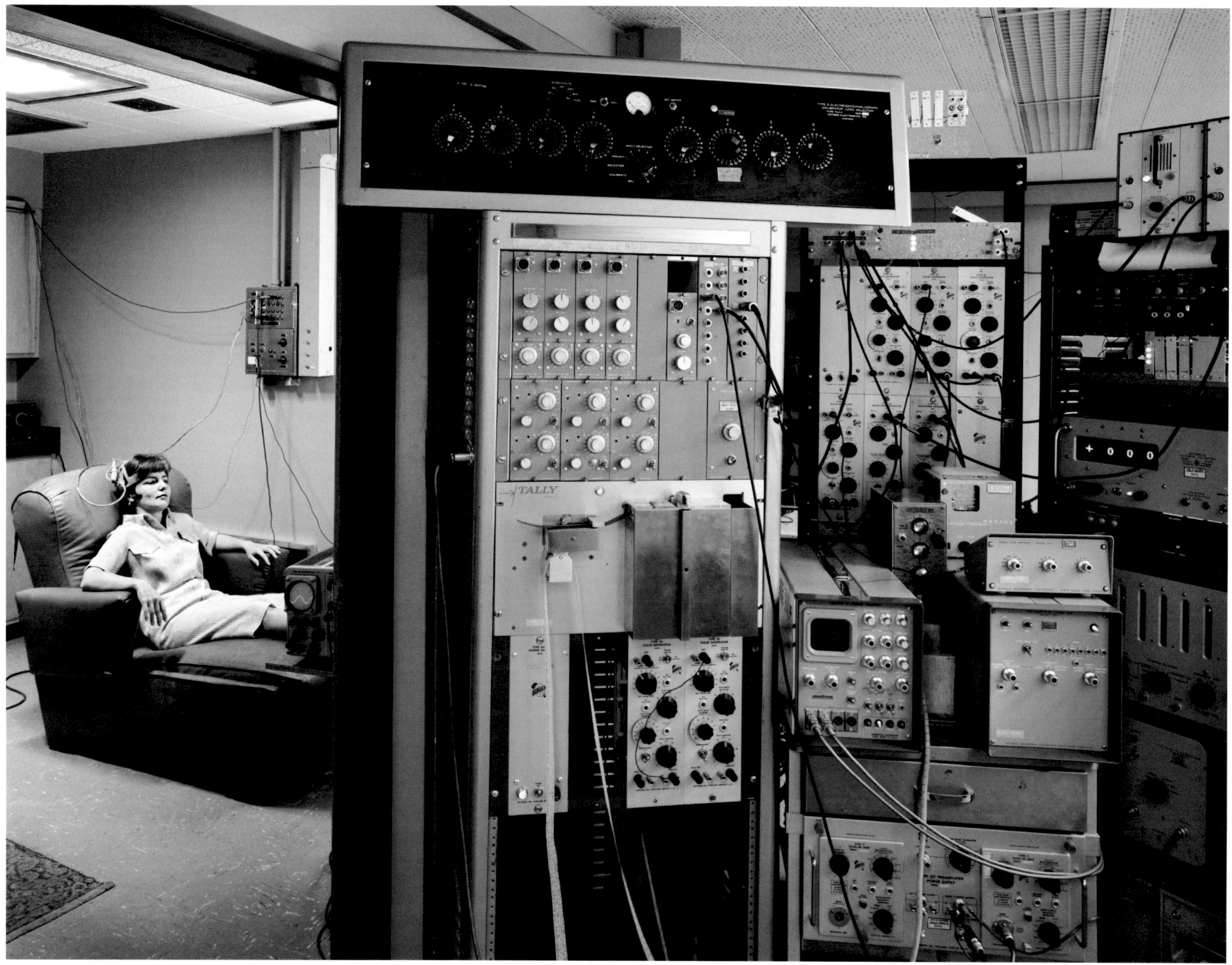

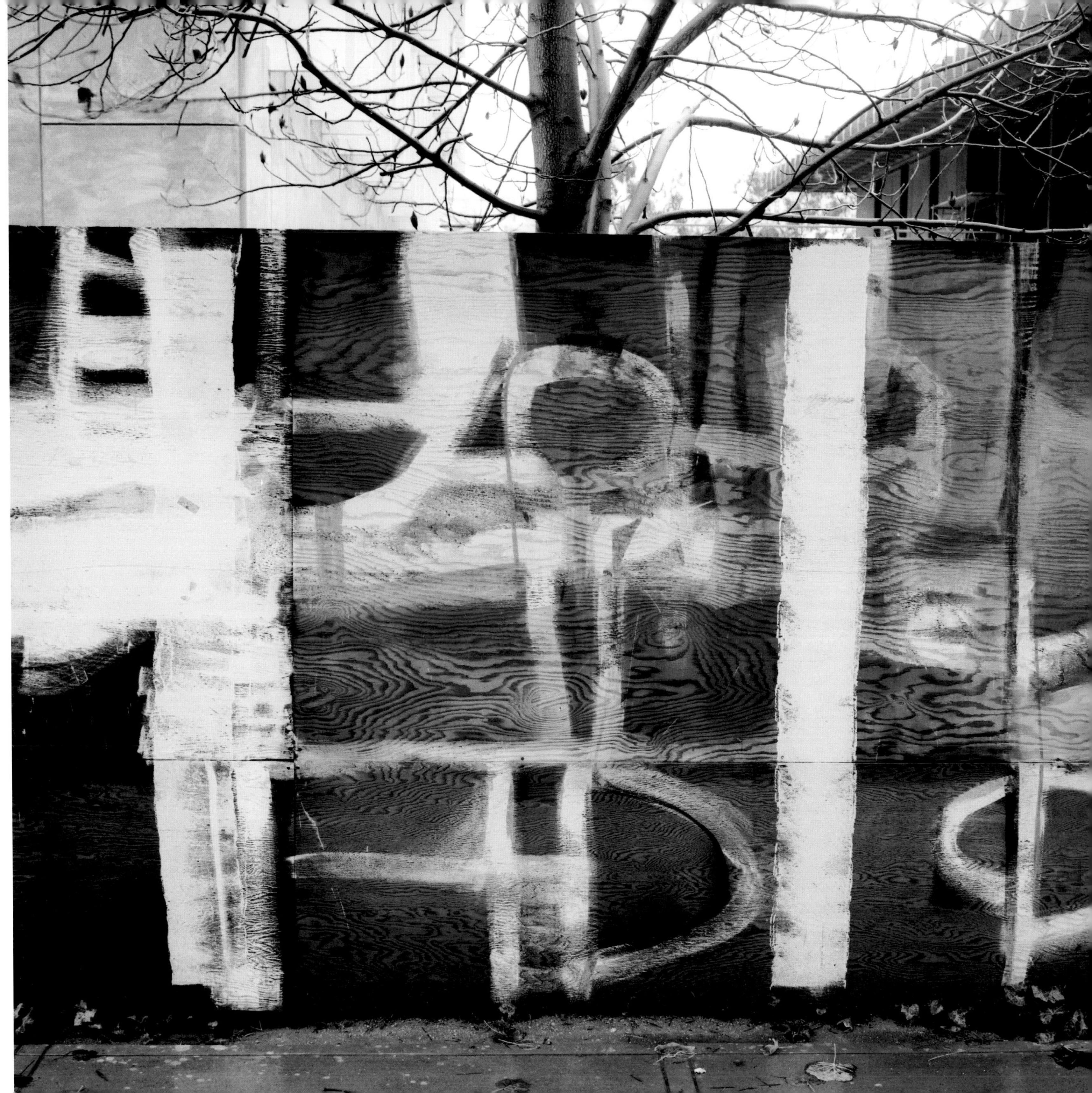

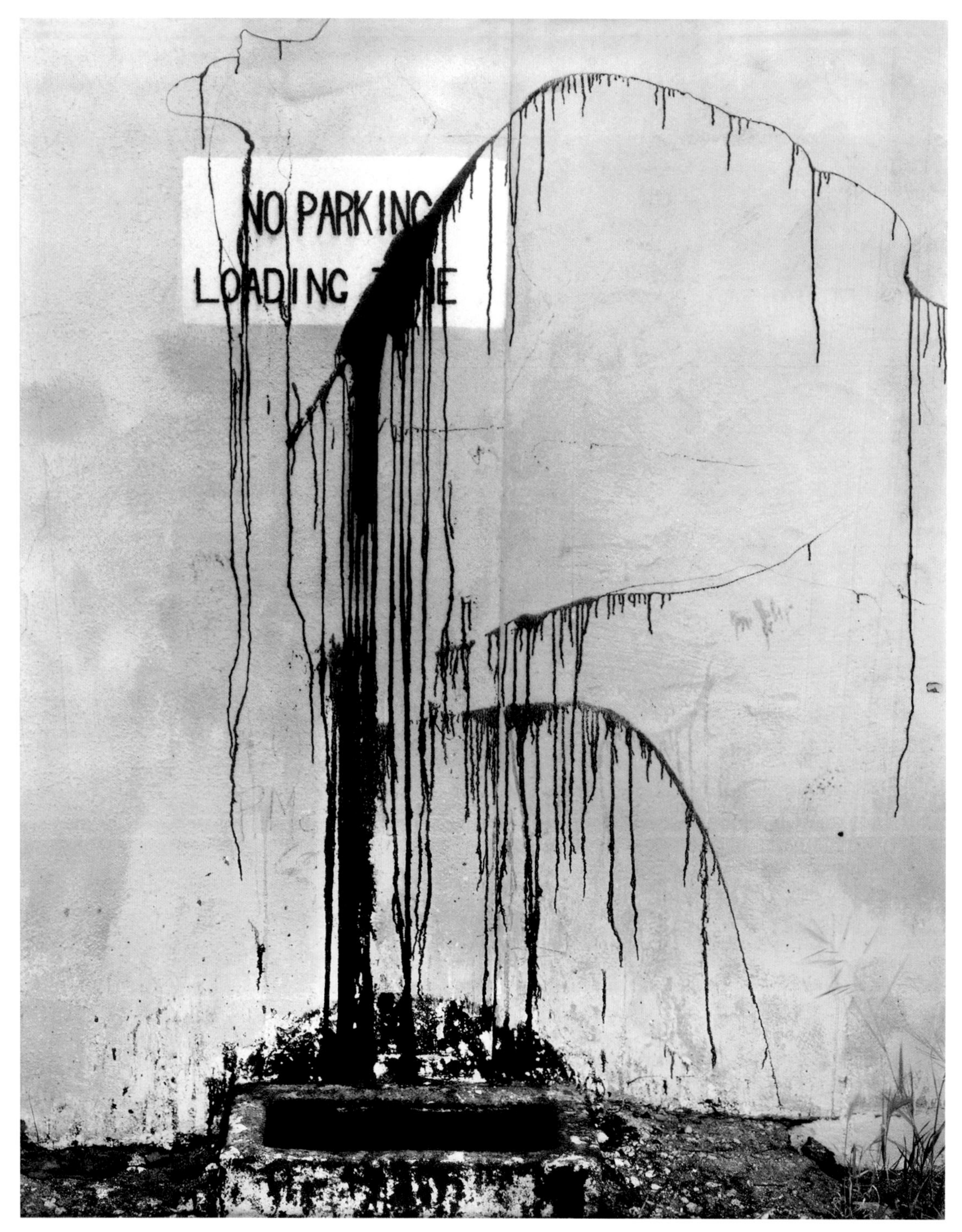

NO PARKING
LOADING ZONE

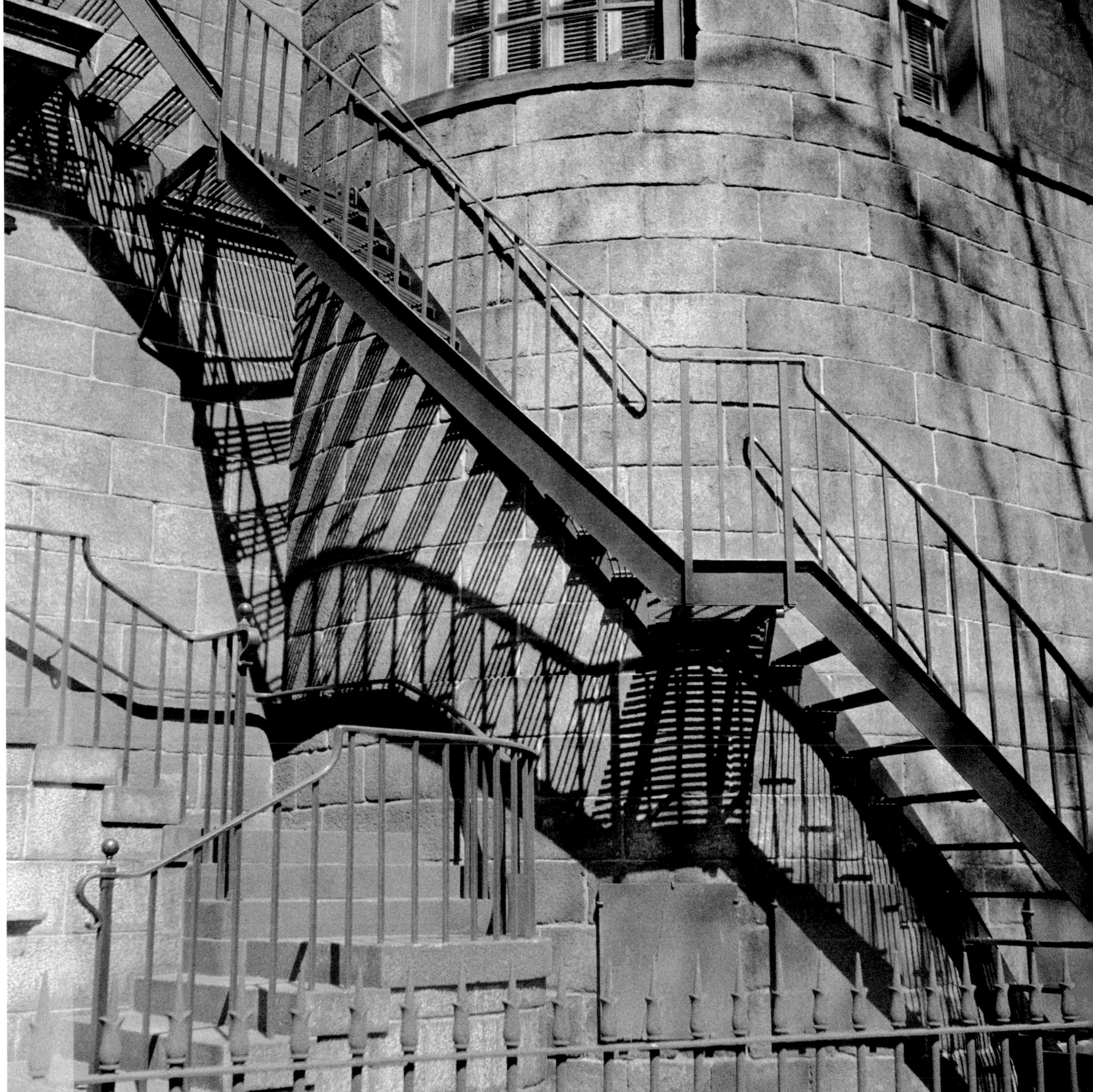

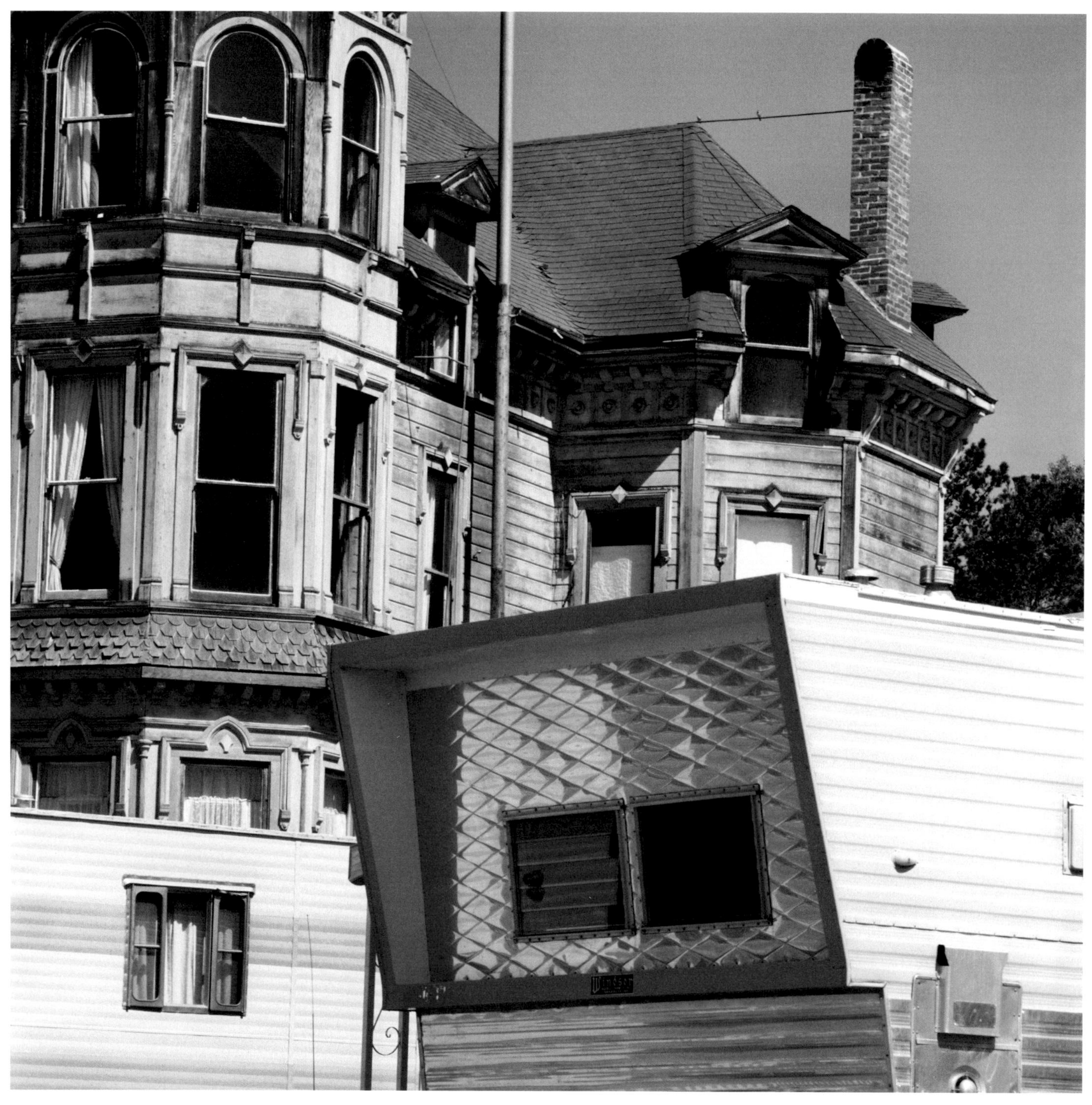

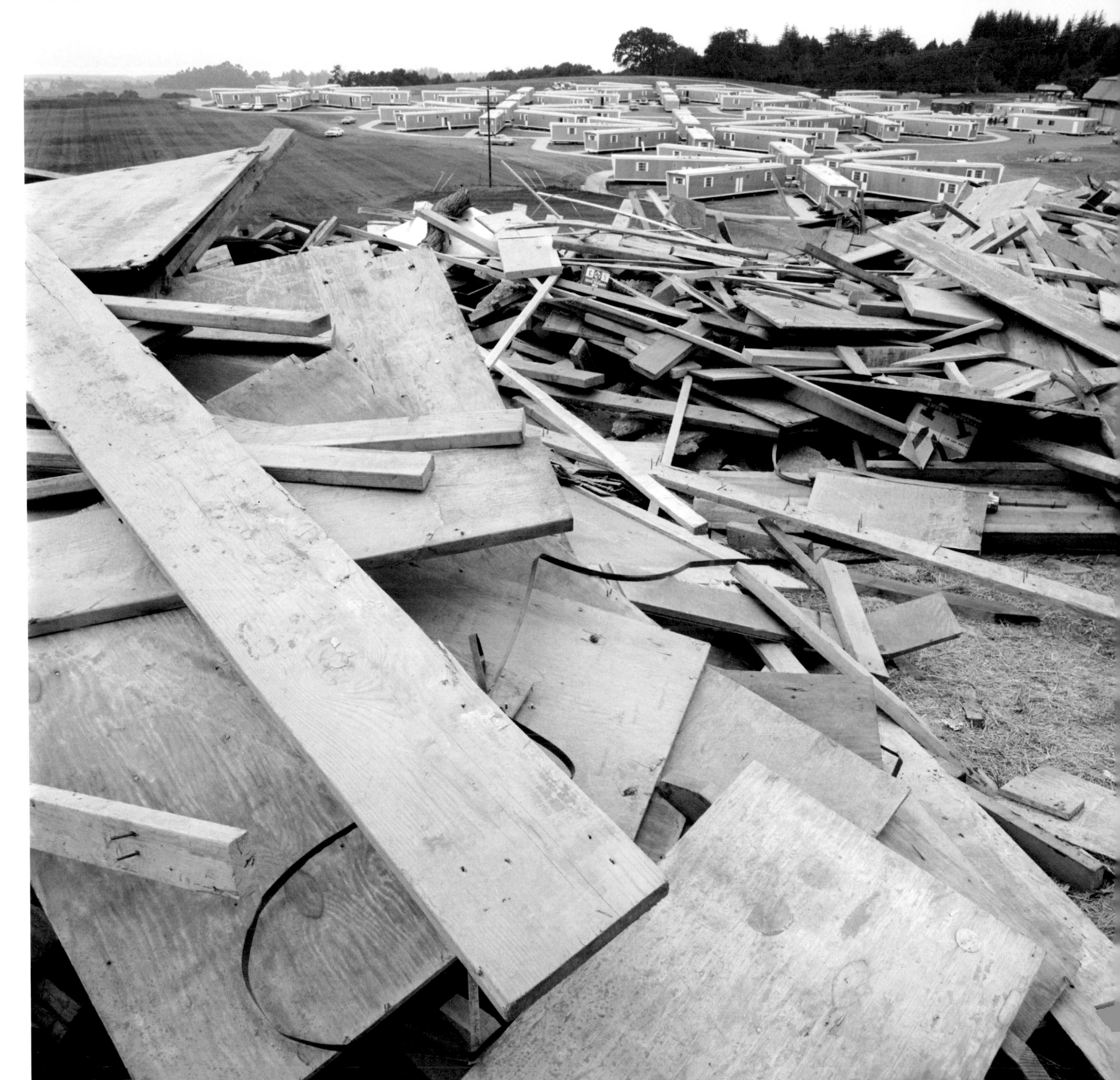

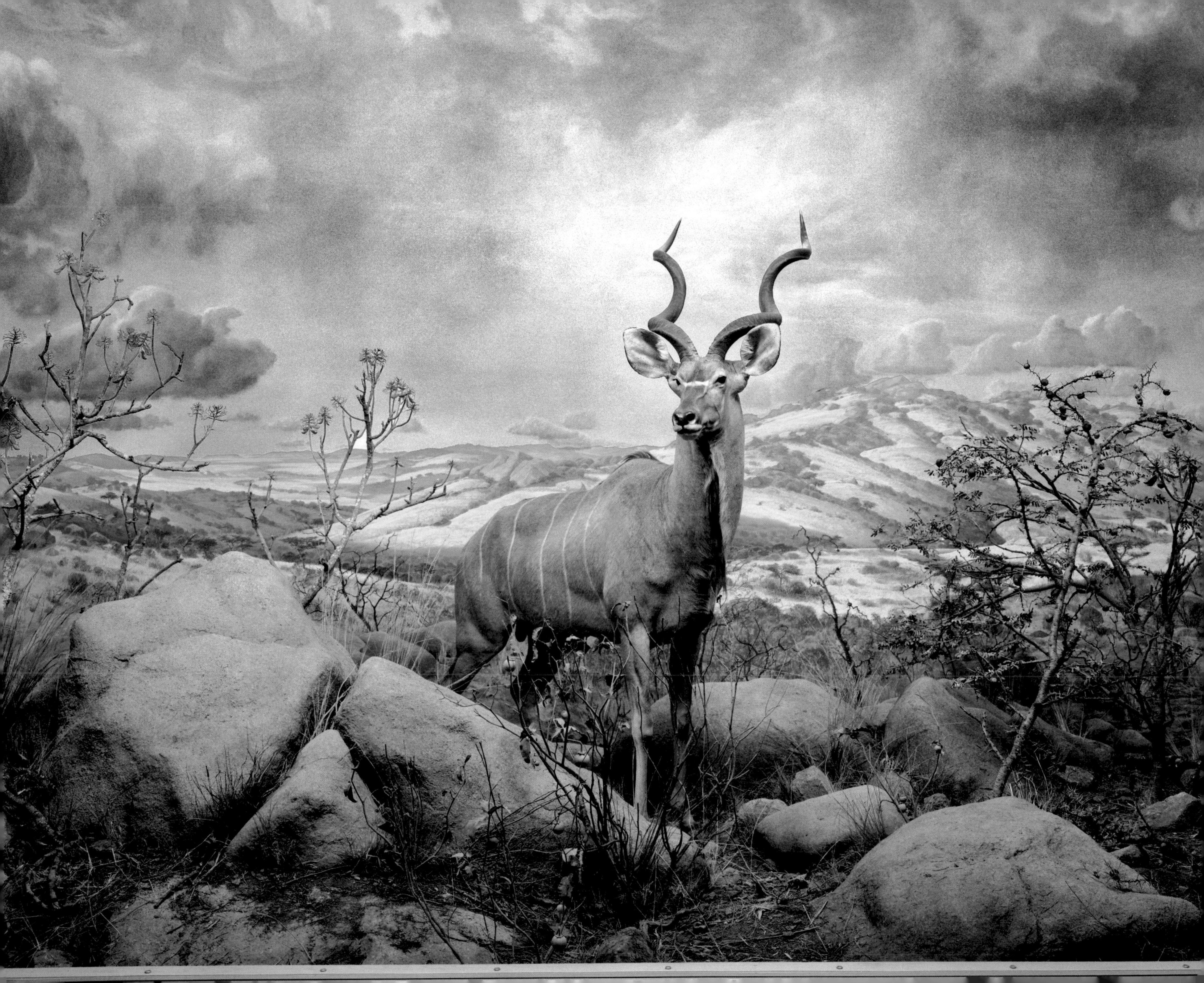

Mike and Ansel

by Erin O'Toole

By the mid-1970s, the national conference of the Society for Photographic Education had become the most anticipated annual gathering for photographers in the United States. The 1975 meeting was a particularly memorable one. It was held at the Asilomar Conference Grounds, a photogenic locale surrounded by cypress trees overlooking Monterey Bay in Pacific Grove, California—an ideal spot for the occasion, given its proximity to Point Lobos, a pilgrimage site for photographers thanks to late local hero Edward Weston. The highlight of the events was a field trip to Weston's former home on Wildcat Hill, where his sons, Brett and Cole, thrilled participants by showing them the negative for their father's iconic *Pepper #30*. For many of the faithful on hand that day, the experience was the photographic equivalent of seeing a piece of the True Cross.

The attendees included Mike Mandel and Ansel Adams, both of whom lived nearby: Adams in Carmel and Mandel in Santa Cruz. The two had met the year before, when Mandel photographed Adams in full catcher's regalia for his *Baseball-Photographer Trading Cards*, a conceptual project that riffed on the fact that photographers like Adams had suddenly become celebrities. Adams's schedule was so busy that Mandel had to book an appointment six weeks in advance to photograph him, but the elder statesman was kind to the young upstart and a good sport, especially after Mandel accidentally underexposed the two rolls of film he shot on their first visit and had to ask Adams for a reshoot. It took another six weeks to get the second meeting on the calendar, but it was worth the wait and the embarrassment. Once Adams signed on to the project, Mandel had an easier time convincing other well-known photographers to participate.

In 1975, Mandel and Adams represented two divergent strains of photography jockeying for prominence. Adams, then seventy-three and arguably the most famous photographer in the country, was an advocate and exemplar of the "straight" tradition, whereas Mandel, then twenty-five, was part of the emerging Postmodernist generation, interested as much in conceptual and appropriation art as in the canonical history of photography that Adams had fought so hard to legitimize. The *Baseball-Photographer Trading Cards,* released to much acclaim later that year, were a testament to the transitions afoot in the field, as established figures of the old guard like Adams, Imogen Cunningham, and Minor White were countenancing renegades charting a new course for the medium such as Lewis Baltz, Robert Heinecken, and Mandel.

According to an account published in the society's journal, *Exposure*, Adams "charmed" the conference with his remarks to the assembled one morning. He also had big news to relay: that he had given his entire archive to the Center for Creative Photography, which would open later that year on the campus of the University of Arizona at Tucson.[1] Mandel was intrigued to hear that by making his archive accessible, Adams intended for other photographers, particularly students, to have an opportunity to "interpret" his work. While Adams likely was referring to his negatives, a select few of which he hoped to make accessible for printing by advanced students under supervision, Mandel had other things in mind. At the time, he and Larry Sultan were in the midst of sourcing strange and enigmatic images from various corporate and government collections, which they would sequence together and publish as *Evidence* in 1977. The thought of similarly combing through Adams's vast archive to find hidden gems to recontextualize in a book was appealing, but ultimately Mandel put the idea in his back pocket and moved on to other things.

Some forty-five years later, as he approached the age Adams was when he made his big announcement at Asilomar, Mandel decided the time was right to revisit the concept of interpreting Adams's work. He made several trips to the Center for Creative Photography, the California Museum of Photography at UC Riverside, and other repositories to see what he might find. Rather than focusing on Adams's majestic landscapes, known around the world, Mandel decided to explore a relatively unknown side of his production, namely the pictures he made for hire. Like most photographers, Adams undertook various kinds of jobs over the years to pay the bills; it was not until late in life that he was able to make a living primarily through print sales and publishing. In addition to leading workshops, he worked for the Curry Company in Yosemite, producing pictures that would illustrate their promotional materials. He shot for magazines, including *Fortune*, and corporate clients like Polaroid, as well as on commission, most notably for the University of California system. Mandel was intrigued by the pictures that most viewers would not identify as having been made by Ansel Adams.

Zone Eleven—the title of which references Adams's famous Zone System for film exposure and development—is an homage tinged with Mandel's absurdist brand of humor. Where the Zone System uses a scale from zero to ten, Mandel suggests that this project somehow goes beyond what Adams sought to measure. Like his 1974 book *Seven Never Before Published Portraits of Edward Weston*, Mandel is here gently tweaking our expectations of a beloved California photographer. He is not making fun of Adams—Mandel has deep respect and admiration for the man and his work. Like other photographers of his generation who studied the medium in art school or at a university, Mandel benefited from Adams's efforts to institutionalize the teaching and exhibition of photography. While he is now best known for his landscape photographs and his advocacy for the Sierra Club and ecological conservation more broadly, Adams worked tirelessly to further the acceptance of photography as a fine art, on a par with painting and sculpture. Among other things, he was instrumental in encouraging the San Francisco Museum of Art (now the San Francisco Museum of Modern Art) to collect photography upon its founding in 1935; in establishing a photography department at New York's Museum of Modern Art in 1939, the first in a major art museum; and in setting up the photography program at the California School for Fine Arts (now the San Francisco Art Institute), the first program dedicated to teaching the medium as a fine art, in 1946. Mandel is a graduate of that very program.

This book is a collaboration of sorts between Mandel and Adams, except that the photographs Mandel selected for inclusion were not sanctioned by Adams for this purpose, and are likely ones he himself never would have chosen. Adams shot the pictures, but Mandel has adopted them and given them new meaning through sequencing. Given his long interest in popular forms of photography, it is not surprising that Mandel chose Adams's commercial work as his subject. These are essentially vernacular pictures that happened to be made by Ansel Adams—totally unlike Adams's best-known photographs, which Mandel terms "unitary," meaning singular pictures that don't depend on what comes before and after. The pictures in *Zone Eleven* are more open, less self-contained. Mandel has seen something special in each of them that others might overlook and transformed them through canny selection and juxtaposition.

The sequence has its own internal logic, whether through formal or narrative association. For example, a cloud of white steam emerging from a smokestack obscures the sun in one picture, which is echoed in the silver face of a locomotive belching out a dark puff of smoke on the facing page. On the following spread, a sign advertising "The Big Five" is coupled with another featuring a random list of five languages, some bigger than others. What these connections mean is up to the viewer to decide, and the narrative charts a wild and unexpected ride with many twists and turns.

Those who are familiar with Adams's practice will immediately notice that while there are precious few people featured in Adams's personal work, this book is full of them: emoting on stage, jumping off diving boards, performing surgery, riding horses, kissing their beloveds. Adams's sense of humor is rarely evident in the photographs we know him for, but here we frequently see a funny side: a portrait of a bearded man in drag, or a telephone pole sprouting out of a man's head as he watches an approaching train. We see contemporary architecture, graffiti, football, cutting-edge technology, crowds—things we know Adams obviously witnessed, but are largely absent from his iconic work.

Compared to *Evidence*, which is cut through with anxiety and a sense of dread, *Zone Eleven* is more up-beat, despite the fact that Adams made the majority of the featured pictures during World War II and the Cold War period that followed. Some of the photographs were made outside the state, but the sequence overall has a midcentury Californian sensibility, expressing hope for the future. It starts with an image of nature, but moves quickly into representations of vigorous physical activity—people enjoying the outdo-ors in the sun, playing sports or otherwise recreating. There are references to the history of the West, and the transformations that took place there after World War II. We see the smokestacks and trains of the old world but also evidence of the heroic new industries that would soon bring untold wealth to the state. We encounter futuristic architecture, exciting scientific discoveries, a trip to Hawaii.

The positive tone is appropriate, as Adams was an inveterate optimist. He believed that that best way to encourage people to conserve the natural world was to show them how beautiful it was, rather than depicting environmental destruction, which he feared would only inspire apathy. His pictures of Japanese Americans in the Manzanar concentration camp, which are featured in the middle of the book, exemplify this. Adams focused not on the harsh conditions under which these Americans were forced to live, or on the injustice of their incarceration, but rather on how they made their prison livable and retained their dignity.

And yet, *Zone Eleven* is not all sunshine and promise. There are flickers of menace at the edges and so-briety at the end. The final passage features machines straight out of *Dr. Strangelove*, surfaces defaced with graffiti, and piles of wood that suggest the aftermath of a natural disaster. The last photograph depicts a solitary stuffed kudu in the African Hall at the California Academy of Sciences. It is surprising that Adams, the conservationist, would photograph a dead animal in a diorama. It is all the more poignant considering that the date written on the negative envelope for the image is December 7, 1941, the day the Japanese bombed Pearl Harbor.

Note
1. Dick Stevens, "The Conference, an Overview," *Exposure* 13, no. 2 (1975): 5.

List of Plates

p. 32   *Window, Campaign Posters, Massachusetts,* 1960. Collection Center for Creative Photography, University of Arizona. © The Ansel Adams Publishing Rights Trust

p. 33   *One of three Lindeman Sisters, performing as a member of the vocal group Las Tapatias, The Ahwahnee Hotel, Yosemite National Park, California,* c. 1930s. Collection Center for Creative Photography, University of Arizona. © The Ansel Adams Publishing Rights Trust

p. 34   *Fun in Camp—the Premier Danseuse, Ernest Arnold, Canadian Rockies,* 1928. Collection Center for Creative Photography, University of Arizona. © The Ansel Adams Publishing Rights Trust

p. 35   *Greek Theatre Performance of "Electra," University of California, Berkeley,* 1966. Sweeney/Rubin Ansel Adams Fiat Lux Collection, California Museum of Photography, University of California, Riverside. © Regents of the University of California

p. 36-37   *Greek Theatre Performance of "Electra," University of California, Berkeley,* 1966. Sweeney/Rubin Ansel Adams Fiat Lux Collection, California Museum of Photography, University of California, Riverside. © Regents of the University of California

p. 38   *Untitled,* n.d. Collection Center for Creative Photography, University of Arizona. © The Ansel Adams Publishing Rights Trust

p. 39   *Old Bedstead, Lost Burro Mine, Death Valley National Park, California,* early 1950s. Collection Center for Creative Photography, University of Arizona. © The Ansel Adams Publishing Rights Trust

p. 41   *Fence Post, Owens Valley, California,* after 1950. Collection Center for Creative Photography, University of Arizona. © The Ansel Adams Publishing Rights Trust

p. 42-43   *Birds on wire, evening, Manzanar War Relocation Center, California,* 1943. Library of Congress, Prints & Photographs Division, Ansel Adams, photographer, LC-DIG-ppprs-00162

p. 44   *Manzanar Relocation Center from tower, Manzanar War Relocation Center, California,* 1943. Library of Congress, Prints & Photographs Division, Ansel Adams, photographer, LC-DIG-ppprs-00199

p. 45   *C.T. Hibino, artist, Manzanar War Relocation Center, California,* 1943. Library of Congress, Prints & Photographs Division, Ansel Adams, photographer, LC-DIG-ppprs-00240

p. 46   *Teruko Kiyomura, Manzanar War Relocation Center, California,* 1943. Library of Congress, Prints & Photographs Division, Ansel Adams, photographer, LC-DIG-ppprs-00389

Nurse Aiko Hamaguchi, Manzanar War Relocation Center, California, 1943. Library of Congress, Prints & Photographs Division, Ansel Adams, photographer, LC-DIG-ppprs-00007

Tom Kobayashi, Manzanar War Relocation Center, California, 1943. Library of Congress, Prints & Photographs Division, Ansel Adams, photographer, LC-DIG-ppprs-00043

p. 47   *Tatsuo Miyake (student of divinity), Manzanar War Relocation Center, California,* 1943. Library of Congress, Prints & Photographs Division, Ansel Adams, photographer, LC-DIG-ppprs-00090

p. 49   *Tatsuo Miyake, (student of divinity), Manzanar War Relocation Center, California,* 1943. Collection Center for Creative Photography, University of Arizona. © The Ansel Adams Publishing Rights Trust

p. 50-51   *Burning leaves, autumn dawn, Manzanar War Relocation Center, California,* 1943 (detail). Library of Congress, Prints & Photographs Division, Ansel Adams, photographer, LC-DIG-ppprs-00161

p. 52-53   *Rocks and Rapids, Merced River, Yosemite National Park, California,* c. 1955 (detail). Collection Center for Creative Photography, University of Arizona. © The Ansel Adams Publishing Rights Trust

p. 55   *Pinhole Image, Cypress Tree, Point Lobos, California,* 1969. Collection Center for Creative Photography, University of Arizona. © The Ansel Adams Publishing Rights Trust

p. 56   *Tree Shadow on Adobe,* n.d. Collection Center for Creative Photography, University of Arizona. © The Ansel Adams Publishing Rights Trust

p. 56-57   *Physics Lecture Hall Building, University of California, Irvine,* 1966 (detail). Sweeney/Rubin Ansel Adams Fiat Lux Collection, California Museum of Photography, University of California, Riverside. © Regents of the University of California

p. 57   *Fence Painting, University of California, Riverside,* 1966. Sweeney/Rubin Ansel Adams Fiat Lux Collection, California Museum of Photography, University of California, Riverside. © Regents of the University of California

p. 58   *Paul Masson Champagne Cellars, Rotunda, Light Fixture, at Night, Saratoga, California,* c. 1959. Collection Center for Creative Photography, University of Arizona. © The Ansel Adams Publishing Rights Trust

p. 59   *Paul Masson Champagne Cellars, Rotunda, at Night, Saratoga, California,* c. 1959. Collection Center for Creative Photography, University of Arizona. © The Ansel Adams Publishing Rights Trust

p. 60   *White House Ruin, Canyon de Chelly National Monument, Arizona,* after 1950. Collection Center for Creative Photography, University of Arizona. © The Ansel Adams Publishing Rights Trust

p. 60-61   *High Country Crags and Moon, Sunrise, Kings Canyon National Park, California,* c. 1935. Collection Center for Creative Photography, University of Arizona. © The Ansel Adams Publishing Rights Trust

p. 61   *Lick Astronomical Observatory, Mount Hamilton, California,* 1965. Sweeney/Rubin Ansel Adams Fiat Lux Collection, California Museum of Photography, University of California, Riverside. © Regents of the University of California

p. 62   *Rails and Jet Trails, Roseville, California,* c.1953. Collection Center for Creative Photography, University of Arizona. © The Ansel Adams Publishing Rights Trust

p. 63   *Stylized Figures, Art Department Studio, University of California, Davis,* 1967. Sweeney/Rubin Ansel Adams Fiat Lux Collection, California Museum of Photography, University of California, Riverside. © Regents of the University of California

p. 64   *Peter Hamlet, Graduate Student, with Plasma Torch, Chemistry Department, University of California, Los Angeles,* 1966. Sweeney/Rubin Ansel Adams Fiat Lux Collection, California Museum of Photography, University of California, Riverside. © Regents of the University of California

Acknowledgments

I dedicate *Zone Eleven* to Chantal, my wife, for her love, support, and collaboration. And with love to my son, Case, and my daughter, Leyla.

My thanks to Claudia Rice, John Schaefer, and David Vena for their belief in this work and their generous support in enabling me to publish photographs from the Ansel Adams Publishing Rights Trust.

My thanks to Leigh Gleason and Sheila Bergman, UCR ARTS, for their generosity in enabling me to publish photographs from the Sweeney/Rubin Ansel Adams Fiat Lux Collection, California Museum of Photography, University of California, Riverside. Without UCR ARTS' material support, this book would not have been possible.

Leslie Squyres, Rebecca Senf, Anne Breckenridge Barrett, Lee Grissom, and Alexis Peregoy welcomed and guided my research at the Center for Creative Photography, Tucson, Arizona.

Eleonora Pasqui, my editor, and Silvia Pesci, my publisher, at Damiani believed in the work enough to publish it. Lorenzo Tugnoli is responsible for the elegant design.

Erin O'Toole, San Francisco Museum of Modern Art, has contributed a thoughtful essay, *Mike and Ansel*, that provides a critical and historical context to this book.

Michael Szczerban, went out of his way to say yes when he could have easily said no. Sandra Phillips, Curator Emerita of Photography at SFMOMA, has been there for me since the beginning. My thanks to Sharon Helgason Gallagher, President, D.A.P., who has helped me navigate the publishing world with friendship and good humor.

And Alexander Galan, Vidoun Group, who brought Damiani and me together; Enrico Farinazzo for marketing and media outreach; Christina Rice, Senior Librarian, Photo Collection, Los Angeles Public Library; Melissa S. Mead, Archivist, Department of Rare Books and Special Collections, University of Rochester; Patricia Allyn Biggs, Interpretive Ranger, Manzanar National Historic Site; Drew Epstein, Barker, Epstein & Loscocco; Tracey Forsythe, and Chris Dods, First Hawaiian Bank.

In Memory of Larry Sultan, whose insight, intellect, and spirit have enriched my life since *Evidence*.

Zone Eleven

Mike Mandel

photographs by
Ansel Adams

First edition 2021
First printing 2500 copies

Concept, Design and Layout, Mike Mandel
Book Design, Lorenzo Tugnoli
Editor, Eleonora Pasqui

Published by Damiani
info@damianieditore.com
www.damianieditore.com

Printed in June 2021, Italy.

ISBN 978-88-6208-748-3